MONOGRAPHS ON GREENLAND
MEDDELELSER OM GRØNLAND
Vol. 146, no. 3

FACSIMILE
EDITION

Erik Holtved

Archaeological Investigations in the Thule District

Nûgdlît and Comer's Midden

MUSEUM TUSCULANUM PRESS
UNIVERSITY OF COPENHAGEN
2010

Erik Holtved
Archaeological Investigations in the Thule District
Nûgdlît and Comer's Midden

© Museum Tusculanum Press, 2010
Cover design: Erling Lynder
ISBN 978 87 635 1666 2 (Facsimile Edition)

Original print edition, Copenhagen, 1954

Monographs on Greenland | Meddelelser om Grønland
Vol. 146, no. 3
ISSN 0025 6676

www.mtp.dk/MoG

Published with financial support from
The Commission for Scientific Research in Greenland.

Museum Tusculanum Press
University of Copenhagen
126 Njalsgade, DK-2300 Copenhagen S
DENMARK
www.mtp.dk

MEDDELELSER OM GRØNLAND

UDGIVNE AF

KOMMISSIONEN FOR VIDENSKABELIGE UNDERSØGELSER I GRØNLAND

Bd. 146 · Nr. 3

ARCHAEOLOGICAL INVESTIGATIONS IN THE THULE DISTRICT

BY

ERIK HOLTVED

III

NÛGDLÎT

AND COMER'S MIDDEN

WITH 64 FIGURES IN THE TEXT AND 4 PLATES

KØBENHAVN

C. A. REITZELS FORLAG

BIANCO LUNOS BOGTRYKKERI A/S

1954

CONTENTS

	Page
Preface	5
I. Nûgdlît	7
General description	7
Description of the excavated ruins	13
Summer dwellings	45
List of specimens found on Nûgdlît	50
Description of the objects found	61
The cultural and chronological position of Nûgdlît	95
Comparative remarks	100
II. Comer's Midden	107
List of specimens from Comer's Midden, 1947	108
Description of the objects found	112
List of quoted literature	133
List of illustrations	134
Plates	137

PREFACE

The present paper is the result of archaeological researches in the Thule district in 1946—47, including excavations in Comer's midden (Comer A) at the Thule settlement, and at Nûgdlît, an old ruin site which had never been investigated before, situated about 50 kilometers northwest of Thule, a little outside the mouth of Granville Fjord. In addition a preliminary survey was made of a now abandoned settlement, Narssârssuk, about 15 kilometers southwest of Thule. The most interesting results were found at Nûgdlît, where excavations were carried out from the 24th of June to the 24th of July 1947. My assistants at the beginning were MAIGSSÂNGUAQ, who accompanied me to Inglefield Land in 1936, UIVSÂKAVSAK, his wife BIRGITTE, and their little daughter KAVSÂLUK. Later these were succeeded by MITEQ, who as a child had also joined the expedition to Inglefield Land. I owe thanks to all these helpers for their careful and persevering assistance during the sometimes rather strenuous excavation work.

To the grief of all who knew him the young and bold hunter MITEQ later lost his life, when in the winter darkness he broke through the ice with his dog sledge. He had grown up as the adopted son of Maigssánguaq and Avôrtúngiaq, and with his hearty and energetic nature he represented the finest qualities of the Polar Eskimos.

Further I wish to express my thanks to the many Danes and Greenlanders who in various ways have helped me in the work: first of all the manager at Thule, Mr. EGON MØRCH-RASMUSSEN, and his wife AVIAJA; Mag. scient. J. TROELS-SMITH for his hospitable and instructive guidance during a reconnaisance journey in the Disko Bugt, before the final voyage to Thule; and Professor, Dr. A. NOE-NYGAARD who was kind enough to analyse the specimens of iron which were found. Finally I owe special thanks to the Carlsberg Foundation, which by means of a grant has rendered assistance to the completion of the publication.

Søborg   ERIK HOLTVED.

Fig. 1. The Nûgdlît glacier. In the foreground two kayak supports.

I. NÛGDLÎT

General description.

As early as 1936 the existence of old house ruins between Granville Fjord and Booth Fjord was mentioned to me by Polar Eskimos. This is an area where, in former times, people used to fetch pyrites and silicious slate (angmâq) for tools, as indicated by the geographical names Ingneq and Angmârsiorfik. The late Moses Tornge showed me the approximate situation of the ruin sites on a map, as shown in Part I, p. 11, fig. 3[1]), but at that time the name of Nûgdlît was not mentioned. I did not hear this until 1946, when I mentioned my special interest in this area, and was advised to communicate with Uivsâkavsak "whose land it was", i. e. who used to travel there and tend his fox traps. In fact, for some years the place had only seldom been visited by others. Uivsâkavsak cautiously said that "maybe eleven old house ruins might be found out there". He himself, however, had in most cases only visited the place when it was covered with snow, and, as shown on the survey

[1]) I. and II. used in the following will refer to the earlier published parts of the present work, Meddelelser om Grønland Bd. 141, nr. 1—2; 1944.

plan fig. 3, we actually managed to identify with certainty sixty two major or minor ruins—in other words, the largest hitherto known ruin site in Greenland.

The old settlement is situated on the outermost of two low and narrow points which run in a southeasterly direction parallel to the mainland, and thus form two small and shallow bays. The bays are often filled with ice carried in by the tidal current at high water, and lying stranded on the bottom at low water. The name of Nûgdlît means "those living farthest out on the point"—a very apt designation.

The ruin point consists of solid rock, on top of which a $1^1/_2$—2 m layer of gravel and sand, mixed with small, sharp stones has been deposited. The sea cuts in from two sides, and about 200 m from the point of the naze, at house 7 and 8, the land is almost cut through, a strip only about eight meters broad being left. Landwards the ground rises somewhat, at both seaward sides forming steep bluffs from which mighty rocks have been broken away. On the western side the land is undulating, with small lakes in the hollows, and here some vegetation consisting of grasses and flowers can be found. For the rest, the landscape gets its character from the black lichens which cover all the stones. The eastern part rises somewhat more and forms a chaotic field of rocks. From one of the lakes a little creek runs east into the bay. In early summer the water from another lake filters out, soaking the ground, and in these places the *Silene acaulis* (Grl. serfaussat), which in other places is sparse, form a luxuriant blow, glowing in the sun and brightning the rather bare landscape which, in summer time, is often covered by dense fog.

From the head of the two small bays a slightly sloping glaci-fluvial plain leads up to a glacier which, on the sides, is flanked by the higher coastal mountains (fig. 1) whose even surface makes a convenient ascent to the inland ice. In spring, when the sea ice at the mouth of Granville Fjord is broken, this way can be used when travelling "behind" by dog sledge, descending at Iterdlagssuaq and proceeding on the solid ice of the fjord. In fact, we were ourselves forced to take this route when going home after our first visit in the month of May.

The ruins lie in three groups, each having a particular character. The two largest groups lie in the flat area around and just inside the narrowest part of the point. All the house entrances here point to the south or southwest, i. e. towards the sea. The ruins Nos. 1—33 and 52—62 apparently form the older of these two groups, and seem to belong to one continuous period. They were covered by a low vegetation of grass, heather, moss and willow, and in several cases the ruin could only be recognized by a faint depression in the ground.

The ruins Nos. 34—46 are larger, more or less filled with water, and have a luxuriant vegetation of grass. No doubt they belong to a

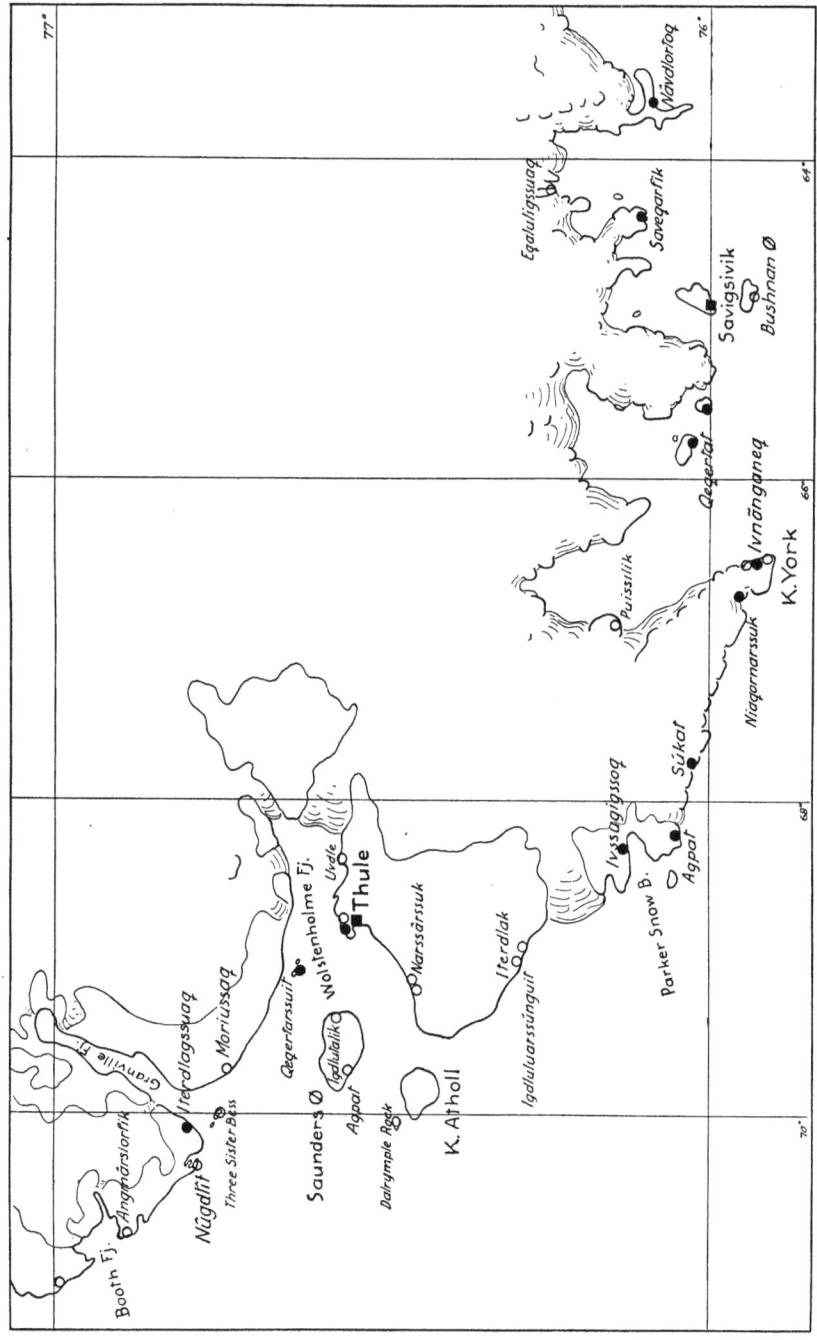

Fig. 2. Map of the Thule area, showing the position of Núgdlit.

later period. Judging by their outer appearance, and compared with similar ruins at Thule, they belong to late Inugsuk, or the "late transitional" period which may be dated at about the 16th century. None of these ruins were excavated because the earthen mounds in front were of such dimensions that the draining off of the water inside would have been impossible in the short time we had at our disposal. Built more or less into these ruins we found three quite new houses with well preserved, high stone walls, sleeping platforms of flat stones, and deep house entrances. Some years ago one of these houses had been inhabited by a man, Tâtiánguarssuaq, who now lived at Thule.

The third group, consisting of the ruins Nos. 47—51, lies about 300 m farther inland on the point, near its northeastern side, where the stony ground begins. The house entrances of this group point southeast, i. e. parallel to the shore which here consists partly of steep cliffs, rather inaccessible in the neighbourhood of the houses. These ruins are quite well preserved, the walls being carefully constructed of stones. They are of a pronounced four-sided type and most of all resembled the ruins at Kap Kent (I. p. 15 ff.). Unfortunately lack of time made it impossible for us to excavate them. It should be done in the future, as no doubt they belong to the oldest habitation of Nûgdlît. Their particular situation affords a strong indication in this respect.

Between the above-mentioned ruins and the shore two pairs of kayak supports made of heavy stones had been erected (fig. 1). Presumably they are of a rather recent date.

In the stony area behind these ruins, towards the head of the bay, we found a great number of stone constructions which in all likelihood were used as meat caches. To which period they belong could not be decided. To judge from the lichen growth most of them appeared to be very old and untouched through centuries. In one of them I found a human skull and a femur covered in moss, showing that this was a grave. With this single exception no human graves could be found in spite of our careful examination. In Inglefield Land, at Marshall Bugt, similar circumstances were met with. In both places, considering the great number of ruins, this deserves notice. It looks as if the custom of burying the dead in solid stone chambers had not become general, at least in Greenland, until late Thule and Inugsuk culture.

Towards the shore in the flatter area with the small lakes, some minor stone rings were found. The dimensions of two almost oval rings were a little more than 1×2 m, the stones being about 15—30 cm long (fig. 4. A). These may have been burial places where the corpse was simply laid out; this interpretation, however, being anything but safe.

Situated high upon a naked, windblown knoll, about 60 m from the steep bluff which faces the sea, and about 200 m to the north of

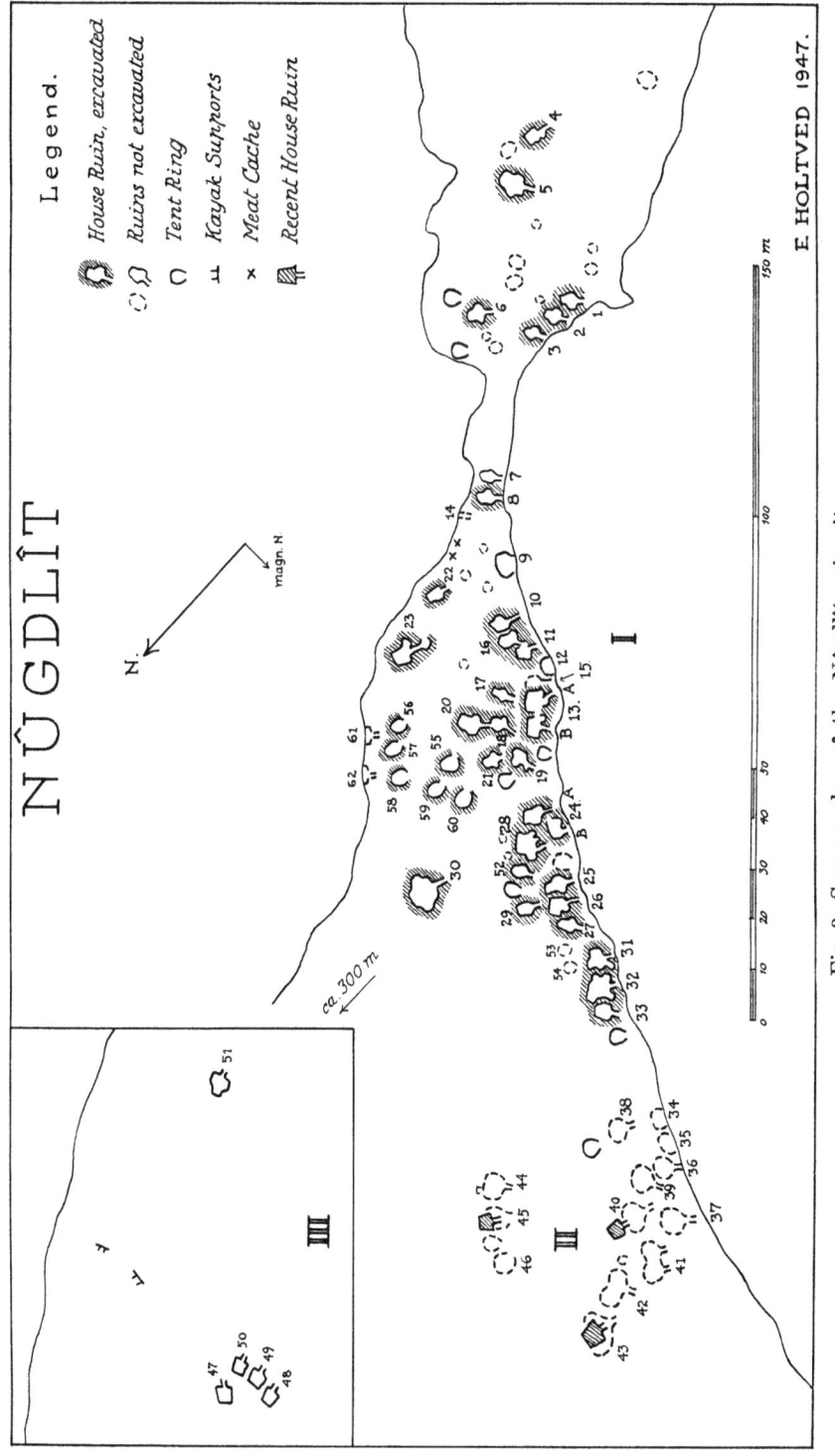

Fig. 3. Survey plan of the Nûgdlît ruin site.

group II, lies the stone ring shown in fig. 4. B. It is almost square, a little more than 2 × 2 m, the rear part being a little narrower than the front, and having a small annex at the north side. Some of the stones are much weathered. It looks like a very old tent ring—but if that be the case its situation is extraordinary. Farthest out on the point, were the remnants of a stone fox trap, built on a low, naked rock, and several meat caches, most of them presumably not very old.

After a preliminary survey I decided to concentrate on the excavation of the ruin group lying farthest out to sea, which appeared

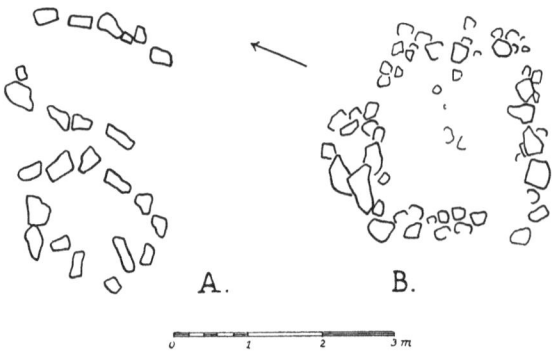

Fig. 4. Stone rings.

to be a connected whole. This decision was made in view of the fact that in the terrain some peculiarities could be seen which I had never noticed before on any ruin site in Greenland. In between the obvious ruins of winter houses were found several faint depressions, which could not have been made by nature, but, which, on the other hand, appeared too inconspicuous to be regarded as house ruins proper. In addition, a very big house ruin is situated alone somewhat behind the other houses. It could hardly be anything but the qagsse, the assembling house of the settlement. Soon it also became apparent that the settlement proved to have close affinities with the western stamped Ruinø outside Inuarfigssuaq in Marshall Bugt, a fact which, of course, stimulated our hope of having this particular culture phase more fully elucidated.

The whole group is situated on rather flat ground, which in places is almost level, the individual houses being dug deep into the ground. In most other places in Greenland, including the two other groups at Nûgdlît, a slightly sloping ground is usually preferred for the semi-subterranean winter houses, but in the group in question this seems to have been felt to be of minor importance. Thus, also the placing of the houses reminded one of the Ruinø, where the houses were found lying on top of the little island on an almost level stretch between the rocks (see I. p. 69, fig. 43). Some of the house ruins near the shore are, to some extent, destroyed by the sea which had washed away the front parts—and of some on the bay side only the house passages were left.

Description of the excavated ruins.

Houses 1, 2 and 3.

(Plan fig. 5). These three houses are the most southern ones, lying on the shore facing the sea. They lie close together but a little displaced in relation to one another. The house passages point southwest, obliquely to the present shore line. Before excavation the ruins appeared as depressions about 30 cm deep, with willow, grass and moss in the bottom. On the sides a few stones were visible, their tops level with the surrounding surface. The house passages were all so damaged that they could only be identified with great difficulty.

House 1 was in the best state of preservation. The wall stones left showed that the house had two rooms at right angles. The extent of the front part, to the east, could not, however, be determined with certainty. The main room, vis a vis the house passage, was closed at the back by a large stone, about one meter long. Immediately in front of this was a platform of earth, 20 cm high and 50 cm wide, covered by a layer of slag, the platform having formed a fire-place. In the western room, in the innermost southwestern corner, was a smaller, niche-like extension with a regular fire-place, lined with stone in the front (fig. 6). In addition another fire-place was found in the house passage itself close to the inner entrance. Only the fire-place on the west side seems to have belonged originally to the house. In particular the large fire-place in the rear of the house, where the main platform was placed, indicates that, at a later period when not regularly inhabited, the house had been used exclusively as a cooking room.—Finds: L3:12032—12035.

House 2 was badly preserved. To judge from the large stones which had slid down from the walls its shape was similar to that of house 1, possibly with a larger extension also at the southeastern side. In the rear part of the main room two stones were standing upright, presumably platform supports. Of the house passage only two high side stones were left, and outside the eastern one, traces of a fire-place could be seen.—Finds: L3:12036—12050.

House 3 was also in a poor state of preservation, but seems to have been of similar shape to house 2. In the eastern room were traces of an apparently secondary fire-place.—Finds: L3:12051—12057.

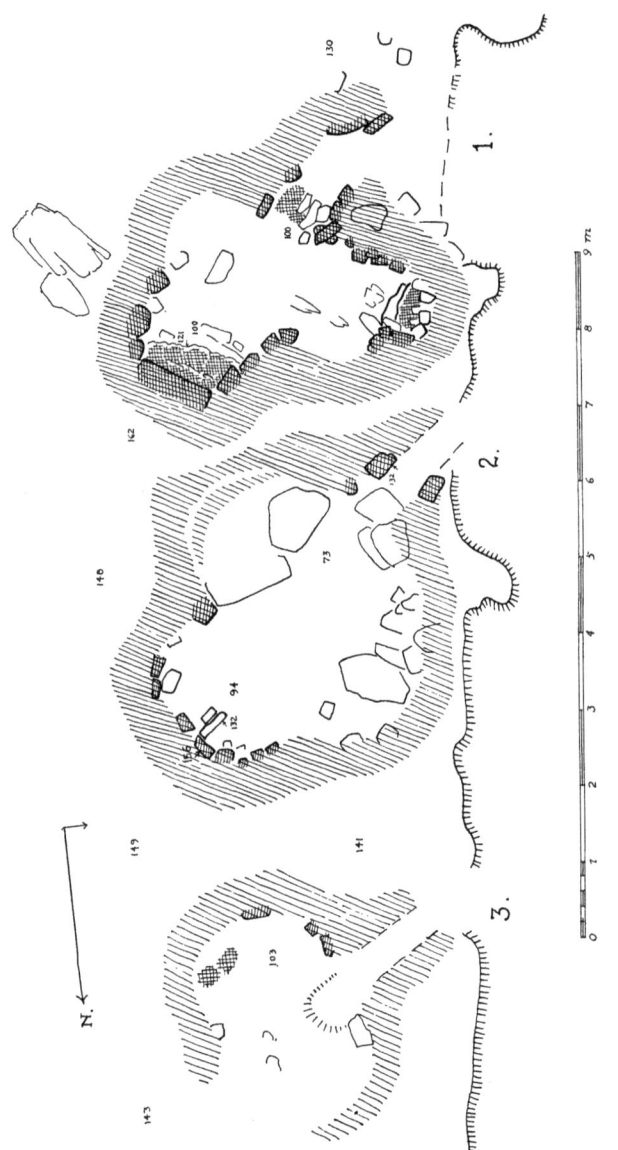

Fig. 5. Plan of house 1, 2 and 3, Nûgdlit.

Fig. 6. Nûgdlît, house 1 after excavation, seen from east.

House 4.

(Plan fig. 7). House 4 lies in the middle of the point, about 30 m southeast of house 1, the house passage pointing south. It is the most southern house in the whole group. Before excavation it formed an irregular depression, about 30 cm deep with vegetation of moss and willow, and several protruding stones. The walls were level with the surroundings (fig. 8). The house proved to be quite well preserved, its dimensions being clearly indicated by the floor paving and the stones in the walls. Some stones have slid, or tumbled over inwards from the western side of the house passage, but their original position could be ascertained. The house is, by and large, square, its inner dimensions being a little more than $2^1/_2$ m × $2^1/_2$ m, with a passage 3 m long leading a little obliquely, to the east of the median line of the house. The passage is deep and semi-subterranean along its whole length. Its exact depth could not be ascertained as it became filled with mire. The floor in the house, lying about 65 cm below the surface outside, was carefully paved with flat stones. At the back the position of the sleeping platform was indicated by stones, about 20 cm high which at the same time formed the partition-wall between two compartments beneath. In the front part of each, a small depression was found, surounded by small, flat stones and filled with blubber, hairs, small bones etc. By the east wall there seems to have been a narrow lamp-platform. To the west of the passage lay the fire-place, to which the approach

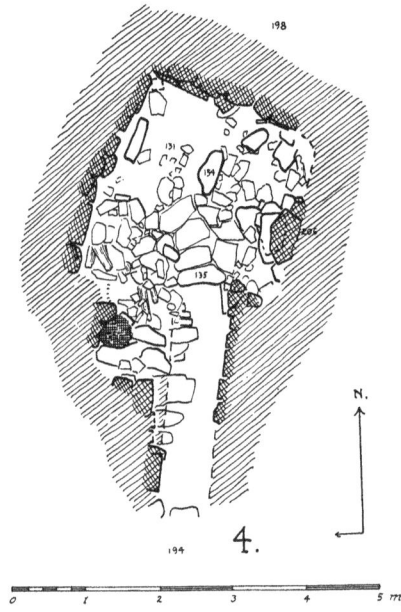

Fig. 7. Plan of house 4, Nûgdlît.

was, apparently, directly from the house. Conditions were less clear in this place, but to judge from the big, upturned wall stones the fireplace had been separated from the passage. In the west corner, near the fire-place, there was an accumulation of smaller flags and stones, but when these were removed a blubber-pit about 30 cm deep and 40 × 40 cm wide appeared in the floor. The floor between the pit and the fire-place was paved, and the whole corner was separated from the rest of the floor by a row of small stones and pieces of whale bones.— Finds: L3:12058—12084.

House 5.

(Plan fig. 9). It lies close behind house 4, with the passage facing southwest. It appeared as a rather large ruin, about 40 cm deep, overgrown with willow and moss and with some stones visible. The top of the walls rose 10—15 cm above the surface. The house had been dug

Fig. 8. Nûgdlît, house 4 before excavation.

down in sand and gravel and was in a rather poor state of preservation. As only a few stones were left in the walls, the ground plan could only

Fig. 9. Plan of house 5, Nûgdlît.

be ascertained approximately. Inside, the house measured about $3^{1}/_{2} \times 4$ m, with its greatest dimension in the direction of the house passage; but in the north side there is an extension, the maximum breadth thus becoming about 4½ m. At the most northerly point of the extension there was a fire-place. In the west corner, near the passage, traces of another fire-place could be seen, as was also the case in house 4. The fire-place in the extension in the north side, however, corresponds to that in house 1. The house passage is about 4 m long and dug down along its whole length.—Finds: L3:12085—12101.

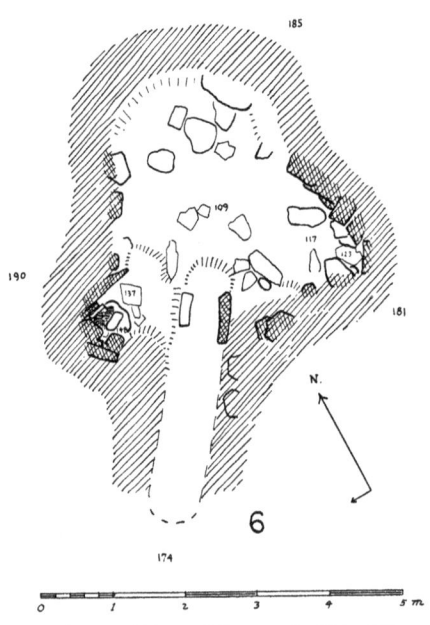

Fig. 10. Plan of house 6, Nûgdlît.

House 6.

(Plan fig. 10). House 6 lies about 10 m behind house 3, and 25 m from house 5. Before excavation it formed a depression almost 70 cm deep with willow and grass on the sides, and moss in the bottom. The walls were level with the surface. In the rear part and in the south side several scattered stones could be seen. The passage points southwest.

The excavation proved that in the rear part of the house no stones were in their original places. Only in an extension in the east side a continuous row of stones was found. Best preserved was the fire-place in the southwest corner, close to the passage, and built into a niche-like room lined with carefully placed flat stones (fig. 11). In front of the fire-place there was one large and a few smaller flat stones. The floor here was about 25 cm higher than the house-floor proper. As in house 4 and 5 the exact nature of the wall construction between the kitchen and the passage could not be ascertained with safety. In house

Fig. 11. Fire-place in house 6, Nûgdlît.

6 there seems to have been no regular stone wall there; but a long stone, which had turned over across the passage way, may have been placed here as a roof support. The passage is about $3^1/_2$ m long and dug down along its entire length. Only a few side stones were still in place.—Finds: L3:12102—12117.

Houses 7, 8 and 9.

(Plan fig. 12). Houses 7 and 8 lie close together on the narrowest part of the point, the passages facing southwest and their outer entrances now terminating in the low brink of the sea. To judge from the position of house 9, which lies close by, and whose passage has been swept away by the sea, the passages of houses 7 and 8 must, in former times, have ended on the level ground somewhat inside the brink and thus have been dug down along their full lengths. Both ruins was filled with sand thrown in by storms. Neither house 7 nor house 9 were excavated.

House 8. — In house 8 a 50 cm deep layer of fine sand was first removed, and below that appeared a culture layer with moss and remains

2*

of baleen. As excavation went on, however, there proved to be more alternating layers of moss and sand, thus indicating that from very early on, sand had been thrown in at long intervals, choking the vegetation which had grown in the meantime. The uppermost layer of sand filling the ruin, was almost without any vegetation, this last filling up

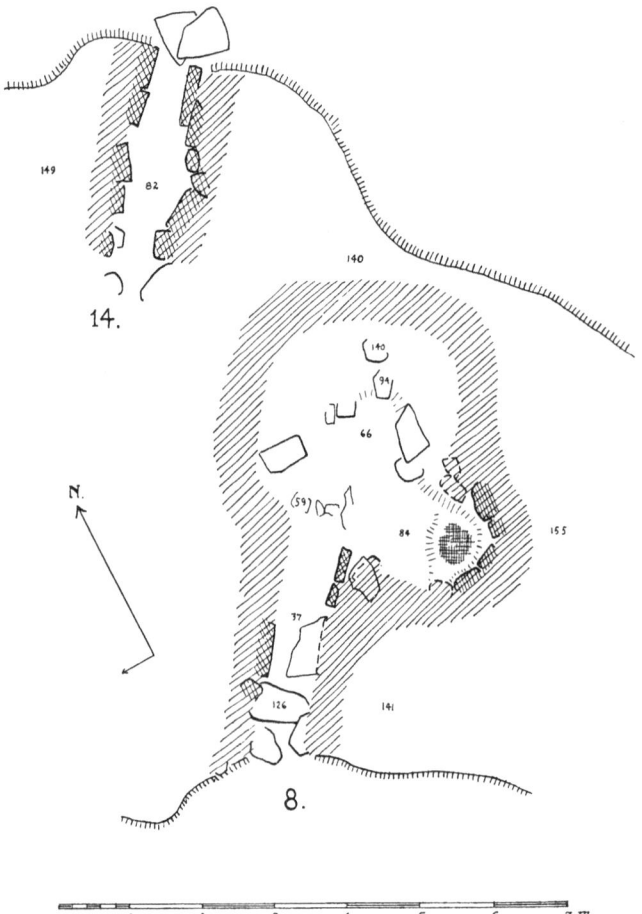

Fig. 12. Nûgdlît. Plan of house 8 and the passage of the swept away house 14.

being presumably of rather recent date. Only a few stones were preserved, except in the passage and in a little extension in the east side of the house, where a fire-place was found. The fire-place and the floor immediately in front of it lie on a level 20—25 cm higher than the house floor. Apart from this extension, the house had been almost square, about $2^1/_2 \times 2^1/_2$ m, possibly with the corners rounded. The length of the passage is about $3^1/_2$ m. The house floor is 70—80 cm below the surface outside, and the bottom of the passage is 30 cm deeper still. Both in the house and in the passage much waste baleen was found, and most of the specimens proper were made of baleen. — Finds: L3:12118—12145.

House 10.

(Plan fig. 13). House 10 is the most southern one in the group of ruins 10—21 which lie close together on a level about 2 m above the

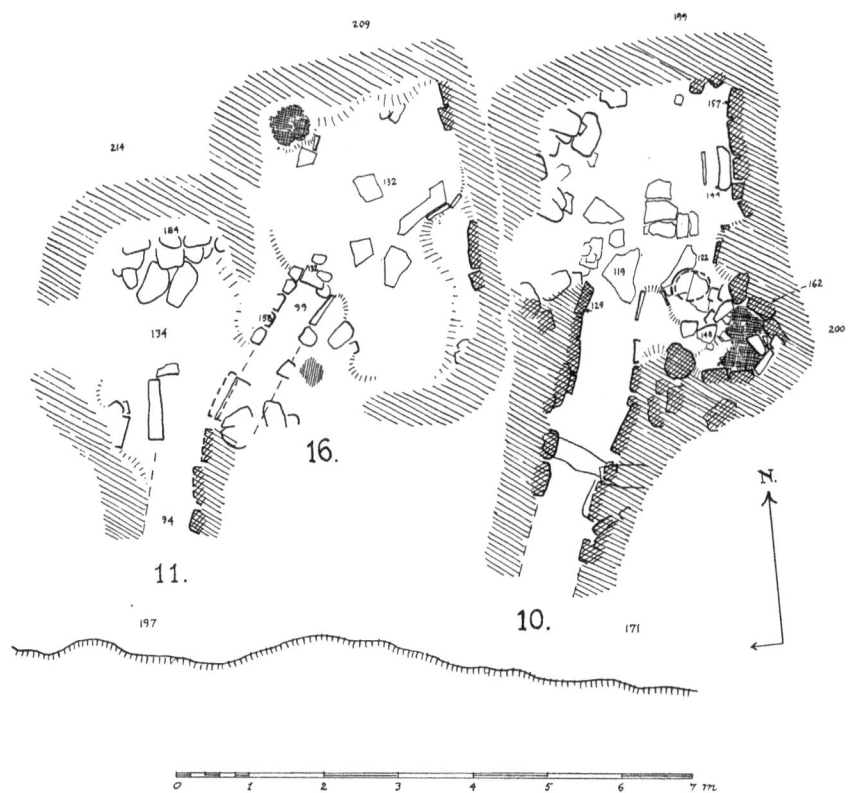

Fig. 13. Plan of houses 10, 11 and 16, Nûgdlît.

high-water line. Before excavation the ruin appeared as a 50 cm deep depression with moss, grass and willow, with several stones, most of them large, protruding. The eastern part of the house and most of the passage were in quite a good state of preservation. The main room is almost square, about 2.7 × 2.7 m, with a large kitchen extension in the southeastern corner. The floor in this part was also a little higher than in the main room, where it was marked by some large flagstones lying 80 cm below the surface. The passage is about 4 m long. Its extension towards the exit could not be exactly determined, but it seems as if the passage did not reach quite out to the brink.

Fig. 14. Nûgdlît, house 10 after excavation.

At the eastern wall of the house there was an oblong stone, about 25 cm high, apparently a platform support. At the back of the kitchen room in the southeast corner a large fire-place, carefully lined with a stone wall was built about 30 cm above the floor in front of it (fig. 14). Between the fire-place and the main room two flat stones had been placed supporting an oval baleen ring, about 50 × 40 cm, which seems to have been used as a blubber container. The delimitation towards the house room was provided by a long stone, one side of which had a carefully fashioned concavity, corresponding to the curvature of the baleen ring. Between the latter and the house passage a narrow passage led from the house to the fire-place. But also in this case the kitchen seems to have opened, at least to some extent, into the house passage. — Finds: L3:12146—12187.

House 11.

(Plan fig. 13). House 11 lies with its passage opening about 5 m to the west of house 10. It was very badly preserved, no doubt because house 16, lying between house 10 and 11, had been partly built into it. It seems to have been of a type similar to house 10. — Finds: L3:12188 —12195.

House 12.

House 12 lies immediately west of house 11. The passage and the front part of the house had been swept away by the sea. This house was not excavated.

House 13.A.

(Plan fig. 15). Together with house 13.B, which lies close to the west of it, house 13.A formed a big, chaotic ruin, ½—1 m deep, with many stones protruding among the vegetation of grass and willow. At the back the walls were level with the ground surface. In the area between the two houses the excavation uncovered a heap of stones,

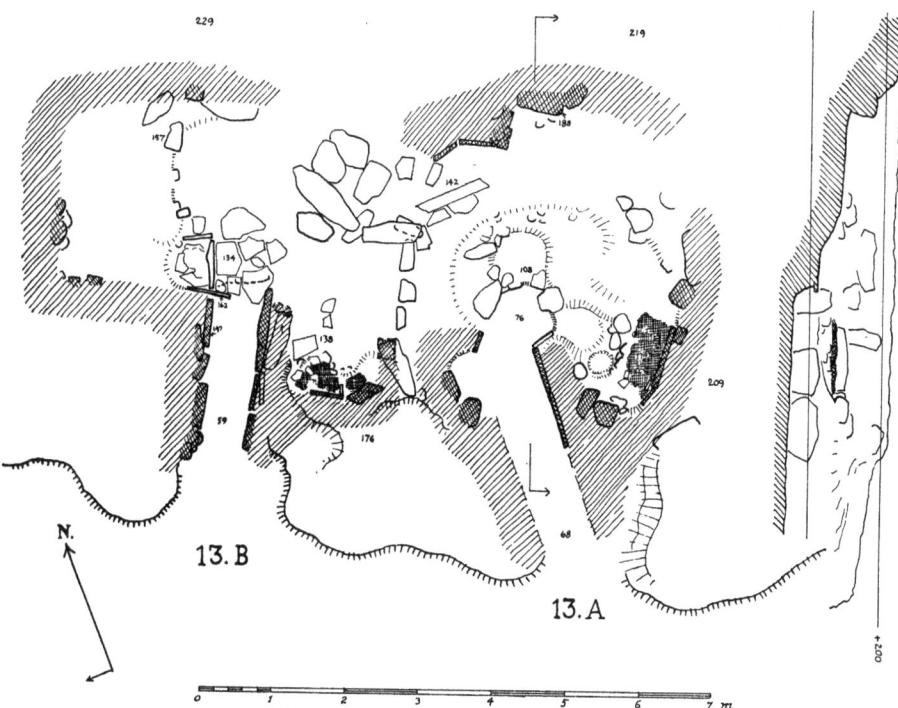

Fig. 15. Plan of houses 13. A and 13. B, Nûgdlît.

some of which were very large, whose original positions could not be determined. Thus here the delimitation of the houses could not be ascertained.

House 13 A had been dug very deep down, the floor level being about 110 cm below the surface, and the bottom of the passage lying 30 cm deeper still. The passage now leads out into the brink, but as this has caved down from time to time, the original arrangement could not be determined. As in other cases mentioned above, it seems most probable that the passage was entered from the level ground which the sea has now washed away. The extension of the house room proper seems to have been about 3 × 3 m. The inner opening of the passage was somewhat inside the front wall, forming a small bend eastward. It looks as if the house floor rose step by step from a narrow, central place just inside the passage, to all sides. No regular pavement was preserved except on the northeast side. Here, however, the flags were placed so high that they more probably belonged to a platform situated in a western extension of the house. The back wall here had a projection at right angles, the main platform having, no doubt, been to the east of it. The delimitation on the east side could not be determined with certainty, but judging by the large number of caved-in stones, there must have been a solid stone wall here. A very large stone, almost one meter in diameter, which had turned over and was lying on the floor, presumably formed the wall between the house room and the kitchen in the southeast corner.

The kitchen extends about $1^1/_2$ m forwards along the passage, from which it was separated by a wall. The fire-place, with a thick layer of slag, takes up all the innermost part of the kitchen. The edge in front is built up of stones, and the back is made of a long, flat stone placed on edge. In front of the fire-place, at its southern end, there was a small pit in the floor. At the side of this, just in front of the fire-place, a few flags had been laid on the same level as the house floor, but between these flags and the innermost, open part of the house passage, a somewhat lower and trodden piece of floor was found, to which the access had, apparently, been directly from the passage. On the east side of the passage, towards the kitchen, some of the side stones were still in place, these being large, flat stones placed on edge. On the west side, near the inner end, there was a small, niche-like extension. — Finds: L3:12196—12249.

House 13.B.

(Plan fig. 15). House 13.B seems to have been built a little into the western part of house 13.A, but as mentioned above, its exact extent here could not be ascertained. On the western side of house 13.B there was a spacious extension, about $1^1/_2 \times 2$ m, and occupied presumably by a sleeping platform, the surface here being about 20 cm higher than the floor in front. The delimitation of the rear part also was not quite certain, but it seems as if the house was very similar to house 13.A. Presumably the big stones shown on the plan partly formed the east wall, and partly the wall towards the kitchen, which in this case also extends forwards along the east side of the passage and is separated from it by a wall. In house 13.B, however, the passage ends at the front wall. The innermost part, a length of about $2^1/_2$ m, was well preserved, with side walls of large, flat stones placed on edge, and a paved floor. Just to the west of the entrance there is a small, rectangular room, delimited by flat stones placed on edge, and which had presumably been used for storing meat. In the kitchen, the fire-place, a little more than one meter wide, was erected on the innermost side of the south wall. The east side of the fire-place was apparently formed by a high stone, square in cross-section. Just outside the kitchen the ground was being washed away by the sea. — Finds: L3:12254 —12300.

House 14.

(Plan fig. 12). Of house 14, which lies close behind house 8, only a remnant of the passage, 3 m long, was left, the rest of the house having been washed away by the sea. Not excavated.

House 15.

House 15 lies behind house 12. House 13.A is, apparently, partly built into it. A passage, which presumably belongs to house 15, could be seen deep down in the brink, filled with ice. Not excavated.

House 16.

(Plan fig. 13). House 16 lies between houses 10 and 11, the house passage crossing the kitchen of house 11. It was very badly preserved, except for the passage which is a little more than 2 m long and points diagonally in the direction of the northeast corner of the house. The house apparently had two rooms, the innermost one having been approximately rectangular, $2 \times 2^1/_2$ m, with a small extension, with a fire-place, in the northwest corner. The other, more southerly room, about 2×2 m, seems to have been at right angles to the former, thus forming a protruding corner, as was also the case in house 13.A. Between the southern room and the passage were found remains of a fire-place, but whether this belonged to house 16 or house 11 could not be determined. The floor of house 16 lies about 75 cm below the surface behind it, and the passage is 30 cm deeper still. — Finds: L3:12301 —12341.

House 17.

(Plan fig. 16). House 17 was a small ruin, 40 cm deep, overgrown with willow and moss, and lying close behind house 13.A, the passage pointing towards it. Only little of the stone walls was left, but the ground plan could be seen to have been almost square, a little more than 2×2 m, with an extension in each of the front corners. In the most western corner there was a pit in the floor. In the southern corner was the fire-place, in front of which there was a kind of receptacle with a pointed bottom, made of flat stone, (as shown on the plan), and presumably intended for blubber oil oozing down from the hearth. — Finds: L3:12342—12379.

House 18.

(Plan fig. 18). House 18 lies behind house 13. B with its passage pointing west. The ruin was 50 cm deep, overgrown with moss and willow. Only the southern part of the house proved to be fairly well preserved, as the passage of house 20, which lies behind, cuts through its north wall. There seems to have been only one, almost square room, about 3×3 m, with a kitchen extension at the south side, close to

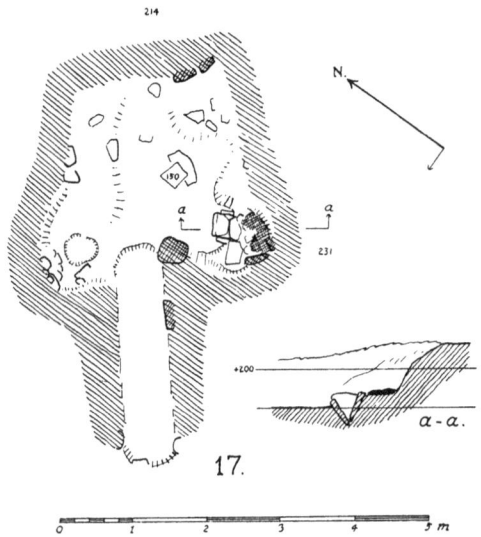

Fig. 16. Plan of house 17, Nûgdlît.

the inner end of the passage. As in house 16, the passage points diagonally in the direction of one of the back corners. It ends a little inside the front wall and, as in house 13. A, there seems to have been direct access to the kitchen from the inner part of the passage. The fire-place is raised about 35 cm above the floor in front of it, and this in turn is a little higher than the house floor proper. Only a few floor stones were found just inside the opening of the passage. The passage is $3^1/_2$ m long. At the outer end its bottom lies 70 cm below the surface, a high stone placed vertically here forming the steep end wall of the entrance. — Finds: L3:12380—12410.

House 19.

(Plan fig. 17). House 19 lies close to, and north of, house 13. B. The ruin was about 50 cm deep, of indeterminable form and overgrown with moss. The excavation proved that it had been almost totally destroyed, and its original form could be little more than guessed at.

It seems to have had an extension in front, at the south side of the passage. At the entrance to this room there was a rounded depression in the floor. In the northern front corner, also, there seems to have been an extension, separated from the passage by a stone wall. About midway along the passage, on its north side, there was a niche-like room with a fire-place. Inside the house no layers of slag could be found. — Finds: L3:12411—12440.

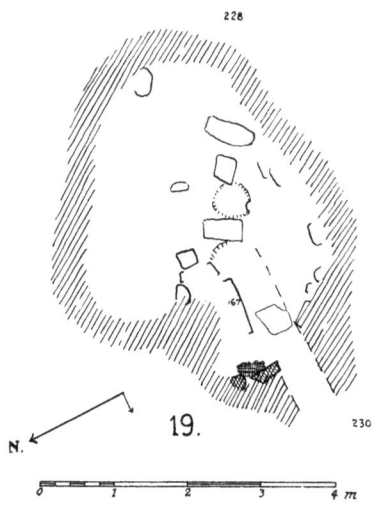

Fig. 17. Plan of house 19, Nûgdlît.

House 20.

(Plan fig. 18). House 20 lies behind house 18, the passage pointing southwest and leading through the wall of house 18. Several caved-in stones could be seen, and the excavation proved that almost nothing of the stone walls was left apart from a few stones in the passage and the fire-place. The house had been almost square, about $3^1/_2 \times 3^1/_2$ m, perhaps with rounded rear corners, and having extensions in the front corners, the southeastern one being occupied by a fire-place. In the other corner a space, presumably for meat, was bounded by stones and by bones, and at the side of this traces could be seen of another, similar arrangement. In, or by the wall were remains of a fire-place, which, however, could not have belonged to the same period as the house; but whether it was more, or less, recent, could not be determined. The fire-place in the southeast corner was carefully built, with a flat stone as an underlayer and stones at three sides. Behind it another layer of slag could be seen, presumably originating from a previous habitation. Toward the back of the house, vis a vis the passage, the main sleeping platform was situated. In front of it there was a pit in the floor, which

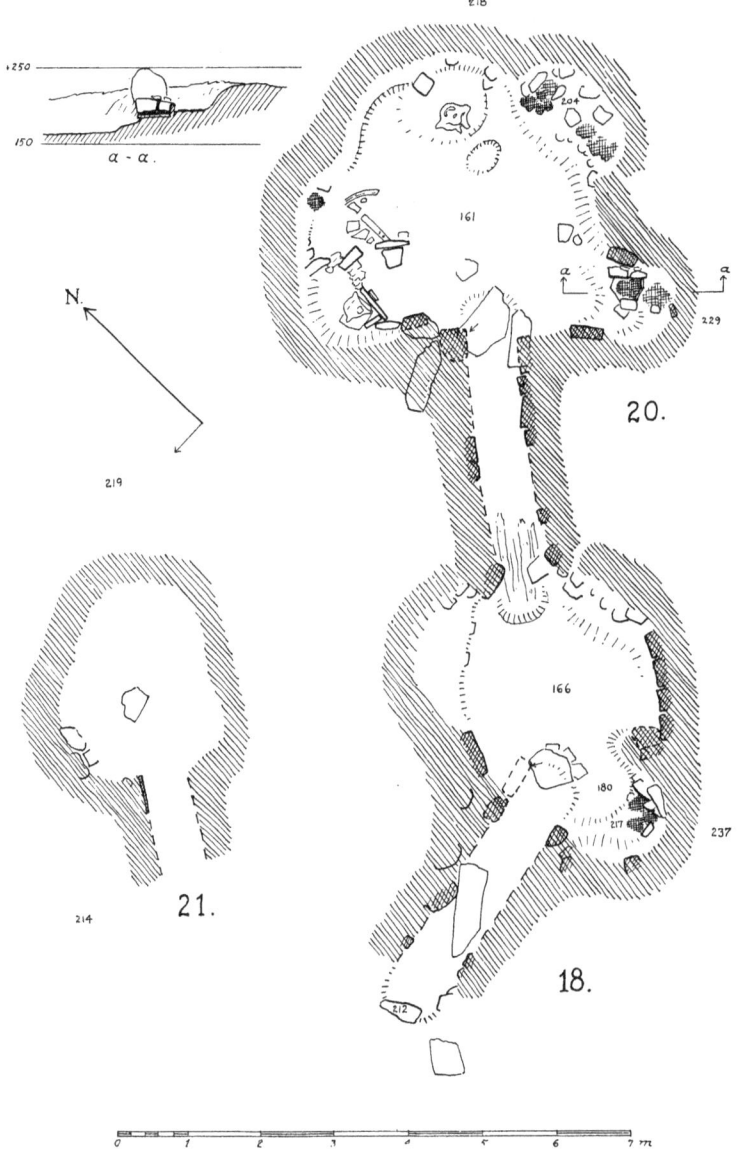

Fig. 18. Plan of houses 18, 20 and 21, Nûgdlît.

here was soaked with blubber oil. The pit was filled with bones, fragments of baleen etc. Inside the pit, where the 'locker' had been, there is also a depression in the gravel floor. Here a large whale vertebra, used as a chopping block, was found.

Towards the back, in the east side of the house, there also proved to be a fire-place, or rather two, very loosely built, only 15 cm below the surface. These can hardly have belonged to the house either, but seem to have been erected later in the abandoned ruin, corresponding to what was found in house 1. The house passage is 4 m long and deeply sunken, the bottom lying about one meter below the surface. In the outer part of the passage several big pieces of baleen had been deposited. — Finds: L3:12441—12491.

House 21.

(Plan fig. 18). House 21 lies close to, and northwest of house 18. Nothing was left of the walls. The house was about $2 \times 2^1/_2$ m with extensions in the front corners. — Finds: L3:12492—12517.

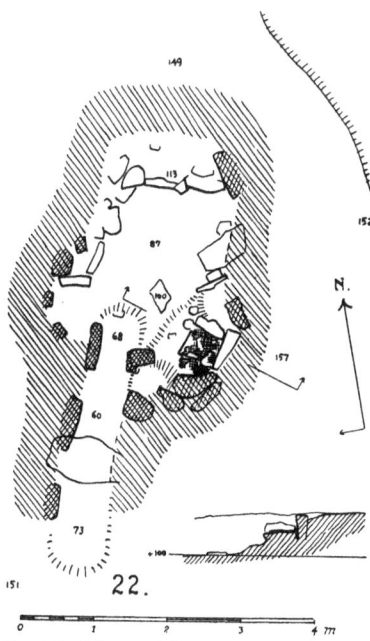

Fig. 19. Plan of house 22, Nûgdlît.

House 22.

(Plan fig. 19). House 22 lies close to the brink of the bay, the passage pointing south. Before excavation the ruin was about 50 cm deep, overgrown with willow. The house proved to be rather well preserved, almost rectangular, 2×3 m. It has a small extension in the southwest corner and a larger one in the southeast corner where the fire-place is situated. Of the platform at the back of the house a row of stones was preserved at its edge, the inner part of the platform having consisted of earth, possibly with flat stones on top. As the row of stones seems, however, to have formed that back wall of a 'locker', it must be presumed that the front part of the platform had originally been made of wood. The fire-place was raised about 30 cm above the house floor and was carefully built with a stone skirting. The floor just in front of the fire-place lies 10 cm higher than the rest of the floor. The passage is 3½ m long. Its floor at the inner end is 30 cm below the house floor, and the outer entrance 75 cm below ground level. — Finds: L3:12518—12539.

House 23.

(Plan fig. 20). House 23 also lies near the brink of the bay, about 10 m behind house 22. The passage points south. The ruin appeared

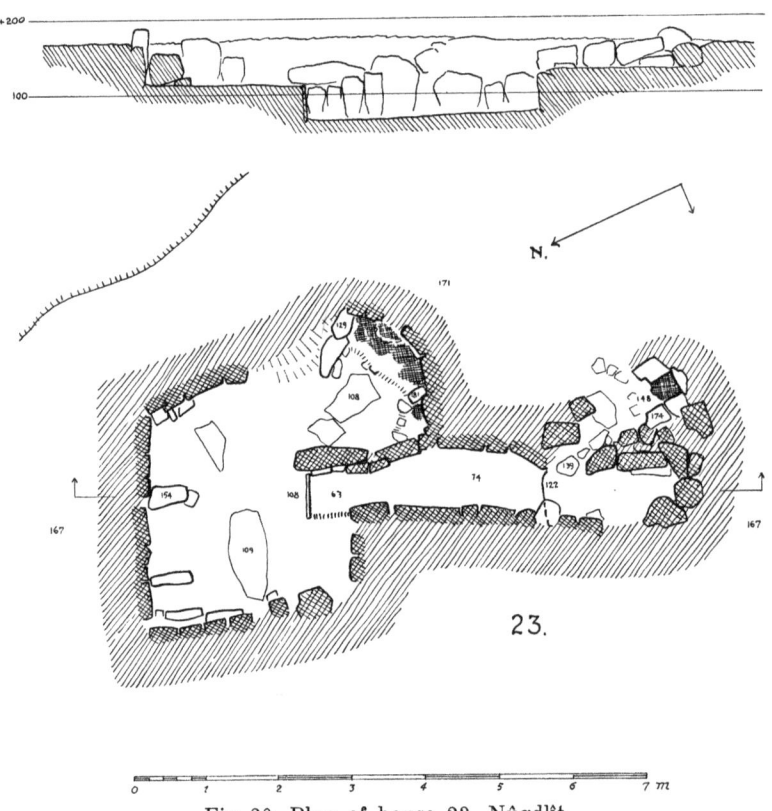

Fig. 20. Plan of house 23, Nûgdlît.

as a depression 60 cm deep, several stones being visible. After excavation the house proved to have been almost square, about 3 × 3 m, but a little skew, and with a kitchen extension in the southeastern part, separated from the passage by a stone wall (fig. 21). The long stone, which on the plan is seen jutting out in front of the passage, had presumably been upright, forming a roof support. At the back of the house some high stones were placed at right angles to the back wall. No doubt they are platform supports and thus prove that the platform had been raised about 50 cm above the floor, which itself lies 60 cm below the surface, the floor level being indicated by two large, flat stones. Besides

Fig. 21. Nûgdlît, house 23 after excavation. View through the passage towards the anteroom. To the left the kitchen.

these only a few flagstones were left in the entrance to the kitchen. Most of the back of the kitchen is occupied by the fire-place, which is raised about 20 cm above the floor in front of it. The house passage is 3 m long, 50—70 cm wide, lying in the median axis of the house and reaching 50 cm inside the front wall. At the inner end there is a flat stone 45 cm high, placed on edge. The sides of the passage are made of very heavy stones, some of them one meter high, and also at the outer end there is a broad, perpendicular stone, 50 cm high, which indicates the depth of the passage.

A feature of particular interest is a stone structure, built in front of the passage and serving as a sort of anteroom which served as the access to the passage. It is 2 × 2 m with a wall of heavy stones. To the west side the wall is a prolongation of the passage, the anteroom thus extending somewhat towards the east, where the entrance had been. A solid wall in the direction of the passage divides the anteroom into two parts, of which the innermost one, just in front of the passage, forms an oblong room, presumably used as a meat store. The room outside the partition wall mainly forms a paved passage, leading in obliquely to the sunken house passage, but farthest out, at the south side of the entrance, there is a solid fire-place. The top of the fire-place lies 20 cm below the surface outside and is almost on the same level as the floor, which slopes down towards the opening of the house passage. In the inner room the gravel floor is about 40 cm below the surface outside. — Finds: L3:12540—12576.

House 24.A.

(Plan fig. 22). This is the most easterly house in the next group of ruins, which lie separated from the former by a narrow strip of land with no ruins. At first it could not be distinguished from house 24.B, as they seemed to form one ruin lying close to the brink of the sea, which is here more than $2^1/_2$ m high. The ruin was overgrown mainly with willow, and was 1 m deep, with walls rising about 20 cm above the surface, and several stones protruding from it.

On excavation, house 24.A proved to be a separate house, with its passage leading out into the brink which here was being rapidly washed away. In consequence the foremost part of the passage was totally destroyed. In the house only a few stones were found in their proper places, except for the fire-place. Thus the form and extension of the house could not be ascertained exactly, but it seems to have been almost square, about 3×3 m, with extensions forwards at both sides of the passage. The east side was drawn a little inwards, towards the inner end of the passage, a kitchen in the southeast corner thus being partitioned off. The innermost part of the passage, for a length of one meter, seems to have been open, with sides of large, flat stones placed upright, their tops level with the house floor. In the corner, to the west of the passage, the floor was raised a little above the rest of the house floor. On the east side, however, in front of the fire-place, the gravel bottom was 15 cm lower, but, a little further forward a few flagstones were on the floor level. The whole east side of the kitchen, about $1^1/_2$ m in length, was occupied by fire-places. The innermost one was carefully built, with a large, flat stone at the bottom, oblong stones at the sides, and a high, flat stone forming the back. By the side of this fire-place a layer of slag was lying directly on the gravel. The whole house had been deeply dug down, the house floor next to the passage being almost one meter below the surface, and the bottom of the inner end of the passage $^1/_2$ m deeper still. — Finds in houses 24.A-B, upper layers: L3:12577—12605. Finds in house 24.A: L3:12606—12636.

House 24.B.

(Plan fig. 22). Almost all stones seem to have been removed from house 24.B, presumably to be used in the houses behind. Only the floor layer conveyed an idea of the limits of the house, which seems to have had its largest extension at right angles to the passage. In the east side there seems to have been an extension forward. No fire-place could be found, however. Most noteworthy was a paving of large, flat stones in the most eastern extremity, on a level 10—12 cm below the rest of the floor, which again was 1.25 m below the surface behind. All the

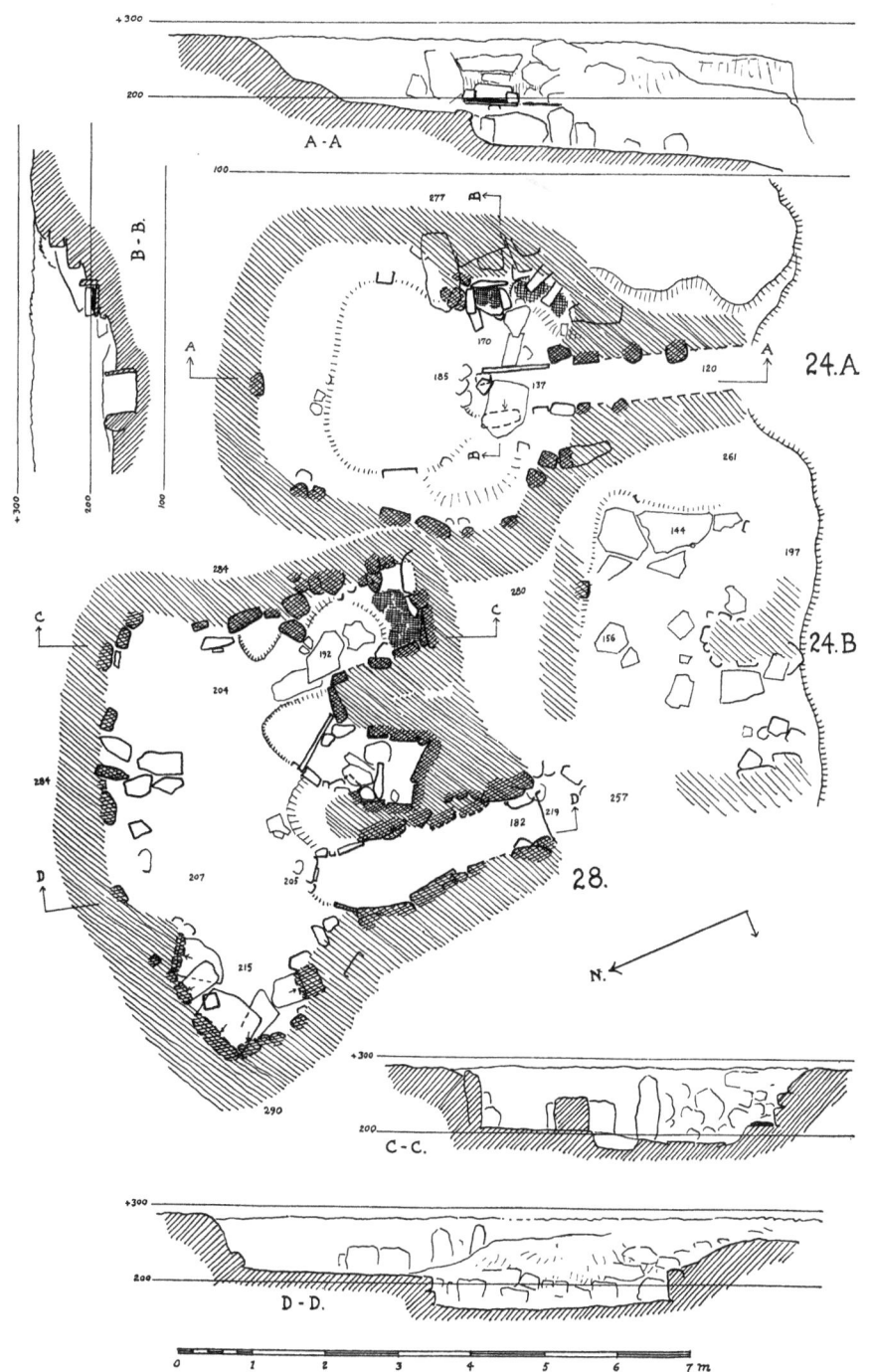

Fig. 22. Plan of house 24.A, 24.B and 28, Nûgdlît.

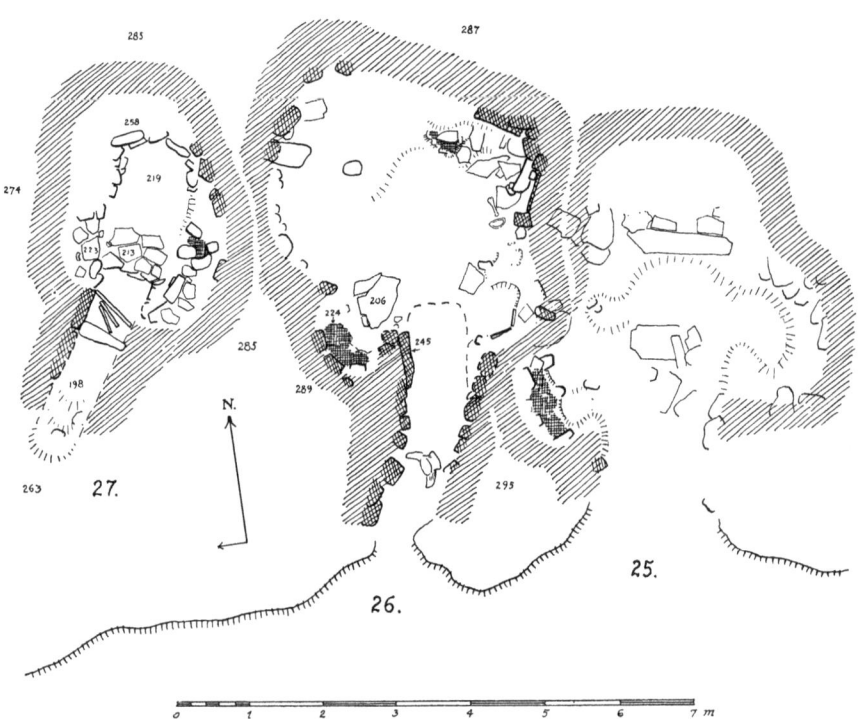

Fig. 23. Plan of houses 25, 26 and 27, Nûgdlît.

passage had been washed away, and not even the place where it had led into the house could be safely ascertained. — Finds: L3:12637 —12675.

House 25.

(Plan fig. 23). House 25 lies about 10 m from house 24.B, out towards the brink. It was much damaged, the whole passage in this case also having been swept away, and the front part of the house being about to slide down. Nothing was left of stone walls proper. The house could, however, be seen to have been nearly rectangular, with a side-room at the east side and an extension with a fire-place in the foremost western corner. — Finds: L3:12676—12688.

House 26.

(Plan fig. 23). House 26 lies close to, and to the west of, house 25, the passage leading towards the brink. It appeared as a depression 20 cm deep, overgrown with willow, and with several stones visible. It soon turned out that only few remains of stone walls were left, and these gave no clear picture of the shape of the house. Further, a culture

Fig. 24. Nûgdlît, house 27 after excavation.

layer spread towards house 25, right under what was presumably the east wall. Apparently several habitations succeeded one another in this place. The shape of the passage also implied that its direction had been changed. On the south side of the ruin, close to the passage, there was a small extension with a fire-place, as in house 25. At the entrance to this kitchen there was a large flag on a level of about 80 cm below the surface outside. At the back of the ruin was a fire-place, which, however, was resting on an older floor layer. One meter east of this fire-place a regularly built stone corner was found. In the whole eastern part of the house the bottom was covered by a thick layer of refuse, cemented by blubber oil, and the uneven gravel bottom below had apparently been much trampled. In the southeast corner, close to the passage, there was a blubber pit in the floor, the southern side of which was made of two stones placed on edge. In this eastern part of the ruin most of the finds were made. — Finds: L3:12689—12805.

House 27.

(Plan fig. 23). House 27, lying not far to the west of house 26, is a small house, about $2^1/_2 \times 2$ m, with the $2^1/_2$ m long passage pointing southwest. No remains of regular stone walls could be seen, but the floor, which, next to the passage, was carefully paved, was on the north and west side bounded by a row of stones which indicate the position of the platform. At the east side there was a small fire-place, and between this and the front wall the space was occupied by a paved platform. In the inner half of the passage the floor was 65 cm below ground level, sloping uniformly upwards from here towards the entrance. The innermost part of the passage was found barred with large, flat stones and seems to have been used, at a later juncture, as a meat cache or the like. Here we found a lot of baleen. — Finds: L3:12806 —12821.

House 28.

(Plan fig. 22). House 28 lies close to, and north of, house 24.B. It was a large ruin, 50 cm deep with many scattered stones, and overgrown with moss and grass in the bottom, and willow on the sides. The walls rose up to a maximum of 20 cm above the surface. The passage points south, the entrance lying just above the northwest corner of house 24.B.

The house proved to have one large room, roughly rectangular, 4 × 3 m, with its largest extension at right angles to the passage, and with a somewhat irregular room, about 1.5 × 1.2 m extending at the western end. From the middle of the back wall, and at right angles to it, a stone wall extended to a length of a little more than one meter. It seems to be the remains of a partition wall which presumably helped to support the roof, at the same time dividing the main room into two parts. The house thus seems to have consisted of three "house-units", of which the most western one is at right angles to the others. The wall of the western room was in part made of very heavy, flat stones which had been placed upright, but now were lying turned over forward, as shown on the plan. The house floor was much trampled everywhere and had no pavement. It lies about 80 cm below ground level.

The passage is about 3 m long and leads into the house near its western side, where it seems to have reached about $^1/_2$ m inside the front wall. The innermost part of the passage was well preserved, with several big side stones in place. Its outer end wall consists of a vertical stone 37 cm high. In front of the entrance remnants were found of a row of stones, presumably the remains of a small anteroom, through which the passage was entered. In the passage were found some pieces of baleen and a large fragment of a gutskin coat.

At the south side the house has two extensions, each about 0.8 × 1.5 m. The more western one, next to the passage, forms an acute angle with the latter and presumably served as a store room for meat and blubber. On fig. 25 it is the one farthest to the right. The innermost part of this room seems to have been separated off by stones lying across it, and in front, it was closed with flat stones placed upright. The bottom was somewhat below the house floor and extended forwards as a pit in the floor, in front of the flat barring stone. In this pit, which

Fig. 25. Kitchen and blubber store in house 28, Nûgdlît.

during excavation was continually filled with water, many specimens and fragments of skins were found.

The eastern extension was the kitchen, with a large fire-place innermost. The entrance to it was flanked by high stones (see fig. 25). In front of the fire-place, on the floor, which was here a little lower than the house floor, a whale scapula was placed on top of a flat stone, while in the entrance and just in front were two large flags. Just in front of the entrance to the kitchen, by the east wall of the house, there was a pit in the floor, which had, most likely, been used for blubber which served as fuel. — Finds: L3:12822—12899.

House 29.

(Plan fig. 26). House 29 lies behind house 26, the passage pointing south. It formed a depression about 20 cm deep with moss in the bottom. Only little of the stone walls was preserved, and the form of the house could not be determined exactly, but its dimensions seem to have been

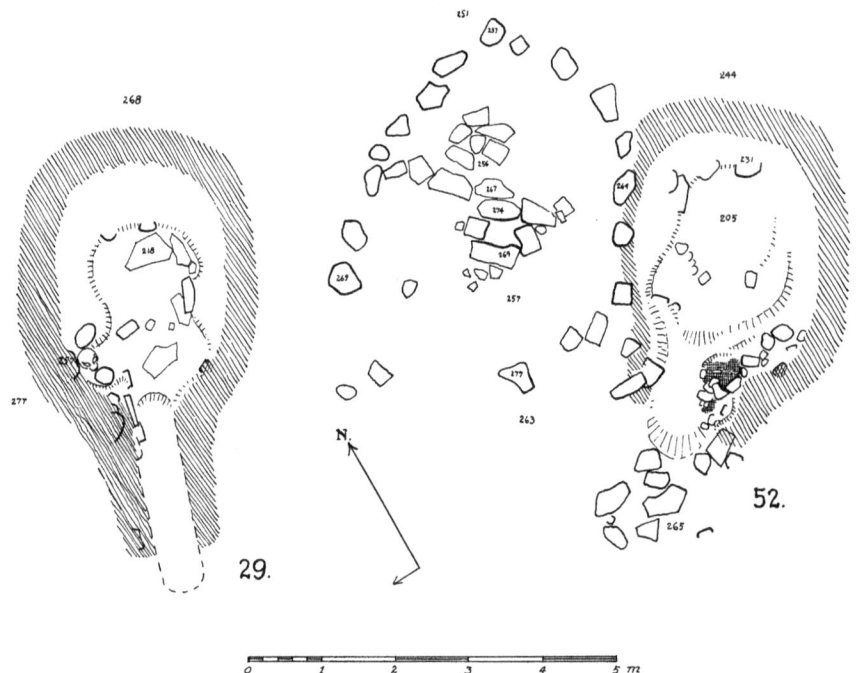

Fig. 26. Plan of house 29 and ruin 52, Nûgdlît.

about $2^1/_2 \times 3$ m, with a passage about $2^1/_2$ m long. Only the limits of the floor could be established fairly well, owing to its thick, trodden culture layer which was surrounded by barren ground, rising in the rear and at the sides. The floor space narrowed in a little at the sides, and possibly the back part had formed the floor of the spaces ('lockers') beneath the platform. Innermost, some flags had been laid. In the foremost western corner there was a niche-like extension also filled up with a culture layer containing several artefacts. On top of this layer a walrus skull was found flanked by two stones, as if it had been "interred" here (fig. 27). To judge from its position on top of the culture layer, however, it must have been deposited during a later habitation, or after the house had been abandoned. About 70 cm from the skull, on the gravel bench, lay a handsome cup-shaped scraper and inside it an ornamented swivel. — Finds: L3:12900—12966.

House 30.

(Plan fig. 28). House 30 lies on the level ground behind the ruin group, about 20 m behind house 28, the passage pointing south. It appeared as a very wide ruin, overgrown with willow and with many stones, some of them large ones, lying scattered about. A slanting stone pillar in the eastern part protruded 1.4 m above the ground. The walls

Fig. 27. Walrus skull in house 29, Nûgdlît.

rose conspicuously above the surface. The whole made a somewhat chaotic impression which did not change during the excavation. To judge from the many overturned stones the house must have had a rather solid stone wall, but only in a few places, on the southwest side. in particular, some more connected remains of a stone wall could be seen. Corresponding to the high stone in the eastern part of the house another was found in the western part, but turned over and broken into two pieces, probably by its fall. These two stones had apparently formed two roof supports, a little more than 1.5 m high. On the floor in front of the passage more long stones lay turned over, but these seem to have belonged to the front wall. Remains of paving can be seen in the area between the two stone pillars (fig. 29). At the back the house seems to have had an extension on each side, the shapes of which, however, could not be ascertained exactly. Apart from these somewhat problematic extensions, the room appears to have been approximately square, about 6 × 6 m. Nowhere were there any traces of a fire-place. The passage leads in at a right angle almost through the middle of the front wall. Its outer end could not be determined with certainty.

Both in its size and arrangement house 30 differed markedly from the other houses, and together with its special position this proves that

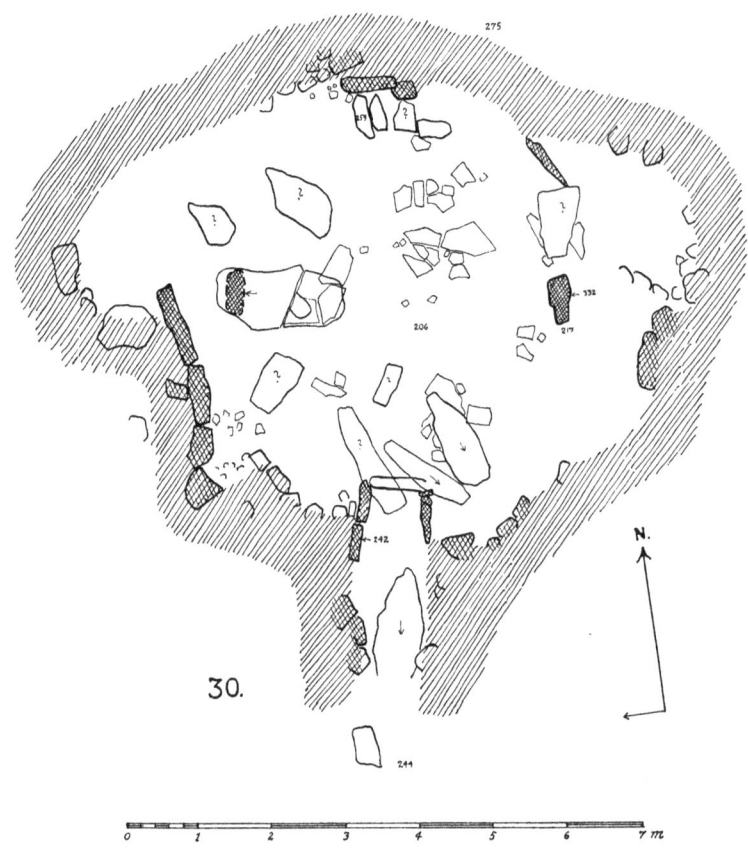

Fig. 28. Plan of house 30, Nûgdlît.

it must have been the assembly house (qagsse) of the settlement. — Finds: L3:12967—13040.

House 31.

(Plan fig. 31). House 31 is the most south-eastern one of the small group of ruins, which include houses 31, 32 and 33. These ruins, overgrown with grass and willow, and lying on the edge of the sea, are the most western houses of the whole excavated group. Most of the passage and the western part of the front wall of house 31 have been washed away by the sea. At the very edge of the bluff the fire-place was still intact, lying innermost in a kitchen room which extended from the southwest corner of the house. Just inside the kitchen, cut off by a little projection of the wall, there was a smaller extension with a 30 cm deep blubber pit. The house had been two-roomed with its rooms at right angles to one another (fig. 30). In the wall the lowest stones were preserved in a few places, and scattered on the floor were the remains

Fig. 29. Nûgdlît, house 30 after excavation.

Fig. 30. Nûgdlît, house 31 after excavation.

of paving. The floor lay about 50 cm below the surface behind it, and the preserved part of the passage was sunken about 75 cm below the floor. — Finds: L3:13041—13070.

House 32.

(Plan fig. 31). House 32 lies immediately west of house 31. Here also most of the passage had been swept away. The ruin was shaped

Fig. 31. Plan of houses 31, 32 and 33, Nûgdlît.

Fig. 32. Nûgdlît. The rear part of house 32 after excavation.

almost like a clover leaf and was about 80 cm deep in the middle. During the excavation an almost rectangular main room, about 3 × 4 m appeared first, the extension of which, on the northwest side, is indicated by the narrow, hatched line on the plan. This main room is joined to a side room on the east side, the total breadth of the house thus becoming about $4^1/_2$ m. Separated off from the side room by a large stone, is a kitchen, about 1.5 × 1.3 m, extending forwards along the passage. Innermost in the kitchen there is a large fire-place. At its east side the fire-place is flanked by a heavy stone, almost one meter broad, the top of which is about 75 cm above the floor in front of the fire-place. On the other side of the passage also, in an extension in the southwest corner of the house, at kitchen was found. Here a large, flat stone formed the bottom of the fire-place. On the north side of the fire-place, and separated from it, there was a small paved space, probably for blubber, which itself was separated from the house by a large, flat stone placed vertically. The bottom of the innermost part of the passage was 70 cm below the part of the house floor next to it. The sides of the passage were made of stones up to one meter high, thus no doubt indicating its full height.

The gravel bottom of the house floor proved to be very uneven, with a few remains of paving. On the east side, however, in front of the side room, there was a greater area of connected paving, and, after a culture layer at the back of the house had been removed, another carefully paved area appeared at the place where the main platform was at first thought to have been. The paving lead in under the stones which were at first assumed to form the boundary of the house. These stones being removed, the pavement proved to extend to a high and broad stone which formed one side of the northwest corner (fig. 32). This was filled with a culture layer, thus proving that the original house had later been made smaller. In the front of the paved area, off the corner at the side room, there was a pit in the floor, filled with bones and refuse and covered by a thin, flat stone. A similar but smaller pit was found a little inside the west wall, the direction of which could not, however, be safely determined.

It was very curious to find a carefully paved space just where the platform ought to be. However, in the annex of house 24.B also an apparently similar arrangement was met with. In the old settlement at Thule many of the ruins had paved rooms under the platforms, but not, as here, forming a continuous floor space. In house 24.B, as in house 32, however, no traces of a platform could be seen. Two possibilities which might be taken into consideration are: that the sleeping platform may have been made of wood and later removed—or, that the sleeping place may have been on the floor itself, as is sometimes the case in Alaska. Admittedly, a thick culture layer was found above the pavement, but this may be due to a cleaning out when the house was made smaller for a new habitation. — Finds: L3:13071—13138.

House 33.

(Plan fig. 31). House 33 is the most western house in the group, lying close to house 32, with its passage to the west. It was in a very bad state of preservation and contained only little of interest. — Finds: L3:13139—13152.

The houses 34—51, belonging to group II and III, were not excavated. House 61 and 62, plan fig. 33, are the remains of two ruins lying on the brink of the bay, farthest to northeast in group I. The passages point southwest. The backs of these houses are being washed away by the sea. Not excavated.

Summer dwellings.

The ruins Nos. 52—60 appeared only as slight depressions in the ground. The excavation proved that they had been dwellings, but of another type than the winter houses described above. They had been partially subterranean, but without a passage. This fact together with their position behind the winter houses indicate that they had been some sort of summer dwellings, apparently of a rather light construction. In most of them traces of fire-places were found. As to the outward appearance and the size of these dwellings nothing can be said for certain, because the ruins merged imperceptibly into the surrounding ground. They have been indicated as ovals on the plans only as a rough estimate. Neither was anything found to give a hint as to how they had been roofed. Most likely the upper part had been a tent-like structure. The extension of the ground-plan seems in most cases to have been about 3×4 m.

Ruin 52, (plan fig. 26), lies immediately to the north of house 28. Several stones were found in the ruin, but the excavation proved that none could be the remains of a stone wall. In the middle of the ruin there is a floor space lying 40 cm below the ground behind it, and skirted by gravel benches. The ruin conveyed the impression of being oval, $2^1/_2 \times 3$ m. Towards the front, at the east side of the entrance there was a fire-place. There was no house passage proper, but only a short passage sloping down from the ground in front. — Finds: L3:13155—13163.

Ruins 53 and *54* lie behind house 31. The excavation of these two small depressions revealed nothing of interest. — Finds in ruin 54: L3:13164—13167.

The group of ruins Nos. 55—60 lie on the level ground between house 23 and house 30, all with their entrances facing south or southeast.

Ruin 55, (plan fig. 34), lies about 5 m north of house 20. It was filled with gravel and stones, including some large ones. The entrance, marked by a few stones at the sides, slopes down to a narrow floor area, about 80 cm wide, which at the front and back lies about 50 cm below ground level, and leads about 2 m inwards. In the middle the floor is raised about 12 cm, and here a few small flags were found. The innermost part of the floor seems to have formed the bottom of a 'locker' skirted by stones, under a platform which presumably had occupied the whole back of the dwelling. Most of the platform had been formed by the gravel surface itself, laid with small, flat stones. On the east side, against a small stone, were found traces of soot, corresponding to the position of the lamp. On the south side, to the west of the entrance, and lying about 15 cm below ground level, a regular stone-edged fire-place had been arranged. The area in front of it seems to have been laid with small, scattered, flat stones, and here also were found spots of soot and slag, most likely originating from the fire-place. Below, on the raised part of the floor also, a layer of slag was found, but here it looked as if there had actually been a fire-place. — Finds: L3:13168—13172.

Ruin 56, (plan fig. 33), lying about 10 m east of ruin 55, formed an almost imperceptible depression in the ground. In the centre as in ruin 55, there proved to be an oblong, sunken area, the middle part of which was raised a little. In the front and back the bottom lay 30—40 cm below the surface. The entrance led in a little obliquely. In ruin 56, however, the sunken floor area had a more irregular boundary associated with some constrictions which in part were skirted with stones. Roughly in the middle there was a large, flat stone, and between it and the entrance several smaller ones. Immediately to the west of the entrance there was a small, regular fire-place, but besides this, some quite small fire-places had been arranged in many places, and without any distinct plan. These were found on the gravel benches, not only on the east and west sides, but also on the north side, where the platform is supposed to have been—and furthermore on the raised part of the floor and inside the 'locker'. To the east of the latter some stones had been placed with their tops level with the ground surface, and against the most northern one there was also a small fire-place. If this has belonged to the original dwelling, the platform must have formed an acute angle with the longitudinal axis of the floor. Yet the small spots of soot on the platform itself remain unexplained, as also, after all, the many small 'toy' fire-places. One is almost tempted to believe that the dwelling had been used as a sort of play house—unless it had served some purposes of cult. — Finds: L3:13173—13182.

Ruin 57, (plan fig. 33) lies immediately northwest of ruin 56. Here also the entrance leads in obliquely. The front part of the sunken floor area is almost circular, about $1^1/_2$ m in diameter, and paved with flat stones. Inside these the floor narrows until it is a little more than one meter in breadth. Right inside remnants of a stone skirting were found. The floor lies 30—40 cm below the surface which rises a little in front. No fire-place proper was found. Only on the west side a flat stone with spots of soot could be seen. At the back a more recent meat-cache had been built on ground level. — Finds: L3:13183—13197.

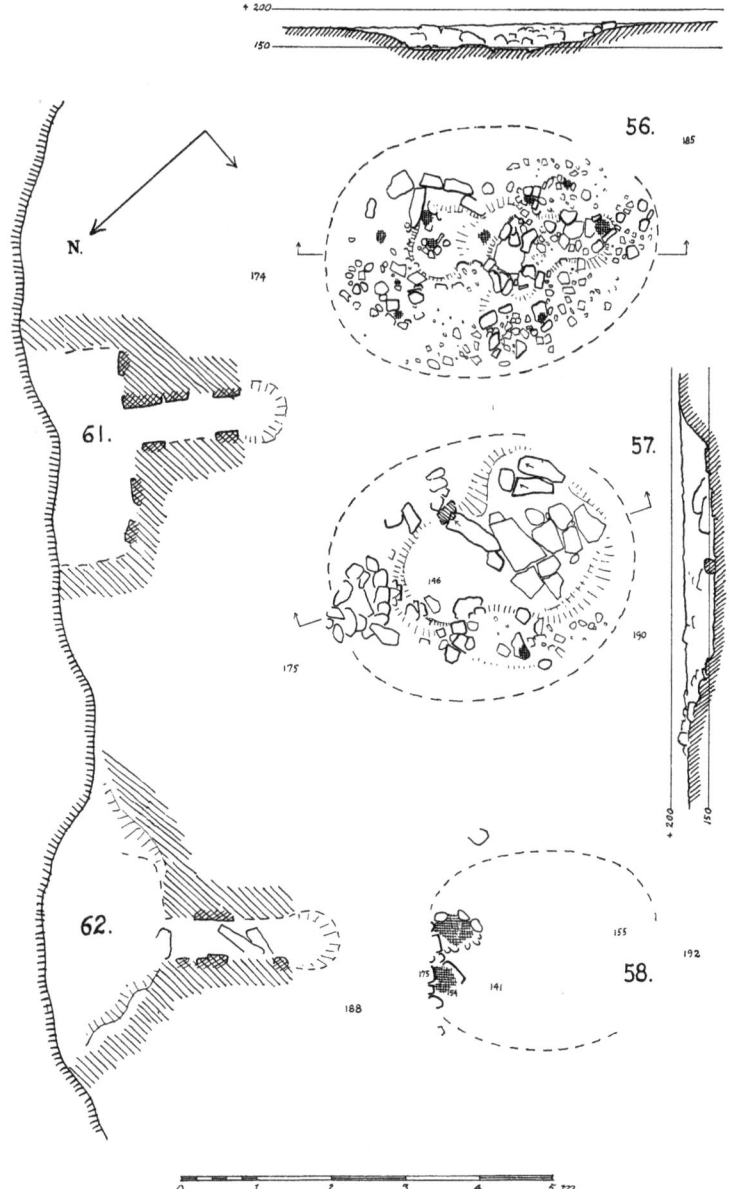

Fig. 33. Nûgdlît. Plan of ruins 56, 57 and 58, and the not excavated ruins nr. 61 and 62.

Ruin 58, (plan fig. 33), lying about 2 m west of ruin 57, proved to have only an even gravel surface. Possibly it had never been a dwelling. Farthest north in the excavated area two fire-places were found close to one another and placed against a row of stones. Thus the place may only have been used as a cooking place. — Finds: L3:13198—13210.

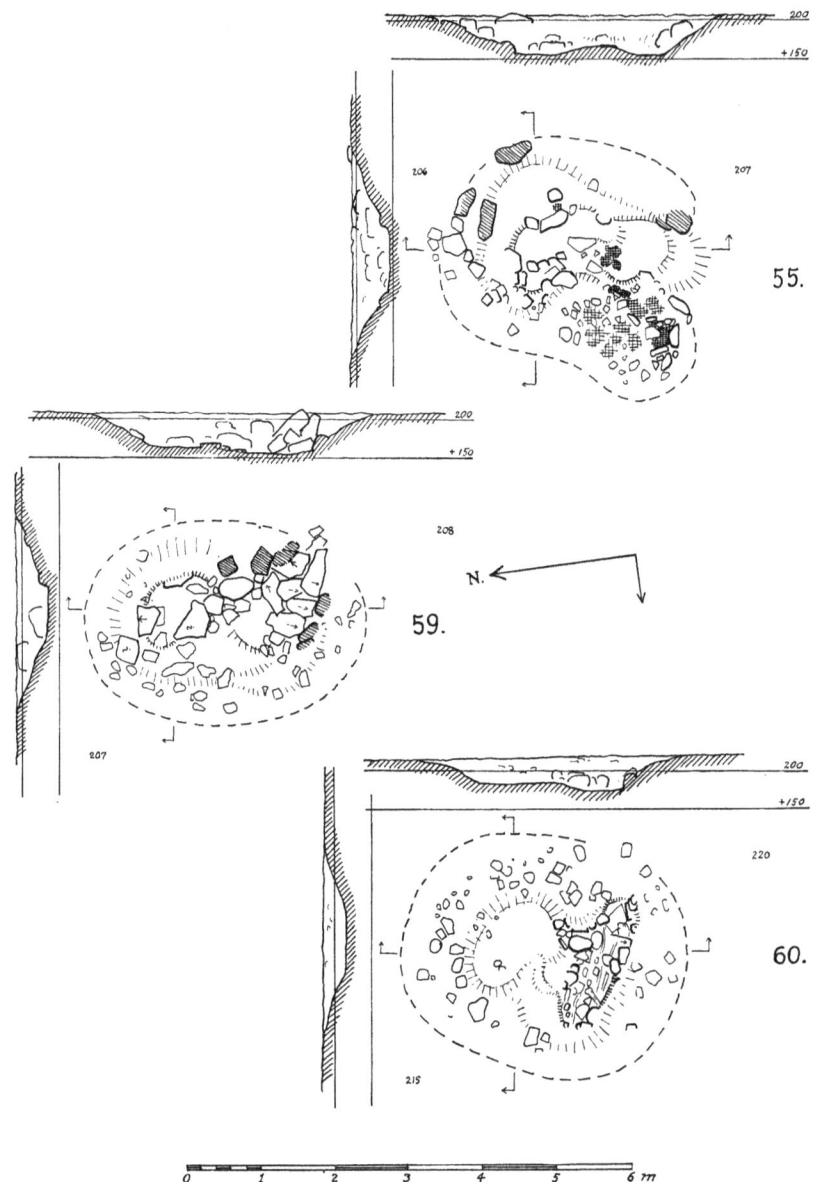

Fig. 34. Plan of ruins 55, 59 and 60, Nûgdlît.

Ruin 59, (plan fig. 34), lies immediately to the north of ruin 55. The entrance leads in obliquely from the southeast. At the entrance a heap of stones about 75 cm long, proves that some kind of solid stone structure had been built here (fig. 35). The sunken floor, which, in front, lies about 50 cm and at the back 40 cm below the surface of the ground, was distinctly indicated by a layer of moss in the bottom, and

Fig. 35. Nûgdlît. Ruin 59 after excavation.

Fig. 36. Nûgdlît. Ruin 60 after excavation.

was furthermore sharply limited by a low step in the gravel. The floor area is widest in front and much narrower in the middle, where it is somewhat raised and paved. The gravel benches on the west side were laid with scattered, small, flat stones. — Finds: L3:13211—13220.

Table 1. List of specimens

	Ref. p.	House 1	House 2	House 3	House 4	House 5	House 6	House 8	House 10	House 11	House 13 A	House 13 B	House 16	House 17
Harpoon Heads:														
Open socket, slots, thin:														
Thule 2, common type	61	..	..	..	..	..	..	..	..	..	..	..	..	..
Fragments	—	..	..	..	..	..	..	..	1	..	..	1	1	..
Vestigial spur	—	..	..	..	..	..	..	..	..	..	..	..	1	..
Thule 3, common type	—	..	..	..	..	..	..	..	..	..	..	..	2	..
Fragments	—	..	..	..	..	..	..	..	..	..	..	..	..	..
Western type (vest. spur)	—	..	..	..	..	..	..	..	..	..	1	..	..	..
Fragment	62	..	..	..	..	..	..	..	..	..	..	..	..	..
Closed socket, thin:														
Oblique spur, blade $\neq$ linehole	62	..	..	..	..	..	..	..	..	..	..	..	..	..
Dorsal spur, blade $\neq$ linehole	—	..	..	..	..	..	..	..	..	..	..	..	..	..
— — blade $\perp$ linehole	—	..	..	..	1	..	..	..	..	..	..	..	..	..
Inugsuk type, fragment	63	..	..	..	..	..	..	..	..	..	..	..	..	..
Swivel, barrel-shaped, special type	—	..	..	..	..	..	..	..	..	..	..	..	..	..
Stopper for harpoon line, spike at one end	—	..	..	..	..	..	..	..	..	..	..	1	..	..
Stopper for harpoon line, spike in the middle	—	..	..	..	..	..	..	..	..	..	..	..	..	..
Mouthpiece for harpoon bladder, oval, flat	—	..	..	..	1	..	..	..	..	..	..	..	..	..
Plug for mouthpiece	—	..	..	..	..	..	..	1	..	..	..	..	..	..
Bone toggle for harpoon bladder	—	..	..	..	..	..	1	..	..	..	..	..	..	..
Mending plug, small	—	..	..	..	..	..	..	..	..	..	..	..	..	..
Movable foreshaft, conical butt, one hole	—	..	1	..	..	..	..	..	..	..	1	..	..	..
Socket piece, with scarf, heavy	64	..	..	1	..	..	..	..	1	..	..	..	..	..
— — small	—	..	..	..	..	..	..	..	..	..	..	..	..	..
— cylindrical, oblong	—	..	..	..	..	..	..	..	..	..	..	..	..	..
Ice pick, triangular butt	—	..	..	..	1	..	..	..	..	..	..	..	..	..
Lance head, movable	—	..	..	..	..	..	..	..	..	..	1	..	..	..
Mouthpiece for the bladder of a bladder dart	65	..	..	..	..	..	..	..	..	..	..	..	..	..
Side prong of a bird dart, barbs on both sides	66	..	..	..	..	..	..	..	..	..	..	..	..	..
Wooden weapon shafts, fragments	—	..	..	..	1	..	..	..	..	1	1	..	3	1
Plug for towing bladder (?)	65	..	..	..	..	..	..	..	..	..	..	..	..	..
Wound pin	—	..	..	..	..	..	..	..	..	..	..	..	..	..
Wooden leg of sealing stool	—	..	..	..	..	..	..	..	..	..	..	..	..	..
Wooden drag line handle	—	..	..	..	..	..	..	..	..	..	..	..	1	..
Line buckle, bear figure	—	..	..	..	..	..	..	..	..	..	..	..	1	..
— bear head	—	..	..	..	..	..	..	..	..	..	..	..	..	..
Toggle, small with oblong hole	—	..	..	..	..	..	..	..	..	..	..	..	1	..
Bow, wood	66	..	..	..	..	..	..	..	1	..	..	..	..	..
— baleen	—	..	..	..	..	..	..	..	..	..	..	..	..	..
Bow brace, bone	—	..	..	..	..	..	..	..	..	..	..	..	..	..

found on Nûgdlît.

House 18	House 19	House 20	House 21	House 22	House 23	House 24 A	House 24 A+B	House 24 B	House 25	House 26	House 27	House 28	House 29	House 30	House 31	House 32	House 33	House 52	House 54	House 55	House 56	House 57	House 58	House 59	House 60
..	..	..	..	..	..	..	..	1	..	1	..	..	..	..	1	..	..	..	..	..	..	..	..	..	..
1	1	..	..	..	1	..	1	..	..	..	..	..	..	..	..	1	..	..	..	..	..	..	..	1	..
..	..	..	..	..	..	..	..	..	..	..	..	..	1	..	..	..	..	..	..	..	..	..	..	..	..
..	..	..	..	2	..	..	..	..	..	..	..	2	..	..	..	..	..	..	..	..	..	..	1	1	..
..	..	..	..	..	..	..	..	..	..	..	..	..	..	..	1	..	1	..	..	..	..	..	..	..	..
..	..	..	..	..	..	..	1	..	..	..	..	..	..	1	..	..	..	..	..	..	..	..	..	..	..
..	..	..	..	..	..	..	..	..	..	..	..	..	..	..	..	..	..	..	..	..	..	..	1	..	..
..	..	..	..	..	..	..	1	..	..	..	..	..	..	..	..	..	..	..	..	..	..	..	..	..	..
..	..	..	2	..	..	..	..	..	..	..	..	..	..	..	..	1	..	..	..	..	..	..	..	..	..
..	..	..	..	..	..	..	1	..	..	..	..	1	..	..	..	..	..	..	..	..	..	..	..	..	..
..	..	..	1	..	..	..	..	..	..	..	..	..	..	..	..	..	..	..	..	..	..	..	..	..	..
..	..	..	..	..	..	..	..	..	..	..	..	..	..	1	..	..	..	..	..	..	..	..	..	..	..
..	..	..	..	..	..	..	..	..	..	..	..	..	..	..	..	1	1	..	..	..	..	..	..	..	..
..	..	..	..	..	..	..	..	..	..	1	..	..	..	..	..	..	..	..	..	..	..	..	..	..	..
..	..	..	..	..	..	..	..	..	..	2	..	1	..	..	..	..	..	..	..	..	..	..	..	..	..
..	1	..	..	..	..	..	3	..	..	..	..	..	..	..	..	..	..	..	..	..	..	..	..	..	..
..	..	..	..	..	..	..	..	..	..	..	..	..	..	..	..	..	..	..	..	..	..	..	..	..	..
..	..	..	..	..	..	..	1	..	..	..	..	..	..	..	..	..	..	..	..	..	..	..	..	..	..
..	..	..	..	..	..	..	..	..	..	..	..	..	..	1	..	..	1	..	..	..	..	..	1	..	..
1	..	..	..	..	..	..	..	..	..	..	..	1	1	1	1	1	..	..	..	..	..	..	..	..	..
..	..	..	..	..	..	..	..	..	..	..	..	1	1	..	..	..	..	..	..	..	..	..	..	..	..
..	..	..	..	..	..	..	..	..	..	..	..	..	1	..	..	..	..	..	..	..	..	..	..	..	..
..	1	1	..	..	1	..	2	..	..	2	..	..	..	1	..	1	..	..	..	..	..	..	..	..	..
1	..	..	..	..	1	..	..	..	..	..	..	..	..	..	1	..	1	..	..	..	..	..	..	..	..
..	..	..	..	..	..	..	..	..	..	1	..	..	..	..	..	..	..	..	..	..	..	..	..	..	..
..	1	..	..	..	..	..	..	..	..	..	..	1	..	..	..	..	..	..	..	..	..	..	..	..	..
..	2	..	..	1	..	1	..	..	..	1	..	..	..	..	1	..	..	..	..	..	..	..	..	..	..
..	..	..	..	..	..	1	..	..	..	..	..	..	..	1	..	..	..	..	..	..	..	..	..	..	..
..	..	..	..	..	..	..	..	..	..	3	..	..	..	..	..	..	..	..	..	..	..	..	..	..	..
..	..	..	1	..	..	..	..	..	..	..	..	..	1	..	..	..	..	..	..	..	..	..	..	..	..
..	..	..	..	..	1	..	..	..	..	1	..	..	..	1	..	..	..	..	..	..	..	..	..	..	..
..	..	..	..	..	..	..	..	..	..	1	..	..	..	..	..	..	..	..	..	..	..	..	..	..	..
..	..	..	..	..	..	..	..	..	..	..	..	..	..	..	..	..	..	..	..	..	..	..	..	..	..
..	..	..	1	..	..	..	..	..	..	2	..	1	..	..	..	..	..	..	..	..	..	..	..	..	..
..	..	..	1	..	..	..	..	..	..	..	..	..	..	..	..	..	..	..	..	..	..	..	..	..	..

Table 1

Ref. p.	House 1	House 2	House 3	House 4	House 5	House 6	House 8	House 10	House 11	House 13 A	House 13 B	House 16	House 17
Bow brace, baleen 66	..	..	..	..	..	..	..	..	..	..	..	..	..
Sinew twister .... —	..	..	..	..	..	..	..	..	..	..	..	..	..
Arrow heads, western type tang:													
Round, pointed .... —	..	..	..	..	..	..	..	..	..	1	..	..	..
Lanceolate, unsymmetrical .... —	..	..	..	..	..	..	..	..	..	..	..	..	..
One barb .... —	..	..	..	..	..	..	..	..	..	..	..	..	..
More barbs .... —	..	..	..	..	..	..	..	..	..	..	..	..	..
Fore end egg-shaped 67	..	..	..	..	..	..	..	..	..	..	..	..	..
Fore end egg-shaped, slit for blade, one barb —	..	..	..	..	..	..	..	..	..	..	1	..	..
Seating for blade .... —	..	..	..	..	..	..	..	..	..	..	..	..	..
Arrow shaft .... —	..	..	..	..	1	..	..	1	..	..	..	..	2
Quiver handle, vertical holes .... —	..	..	..	..	..	..	..	..	..	..	..	..	..
Sling handle, wood .... —	..	..	..	..	..	..	..	..	..	..	..	..	..
— baleen .... —	..	..	..	..	..	..	..	..	..	..	..	1	..
Bola .... —	..	..	..	..	..	..	..	..	..	..	..	..	..
Leister-harpoon head (?), baleen .... —	..	..	..	..	..	..	..	..	..	..	..	1	..
Gull hook with oblique groove .... —	..	..	..	..	..	..	..	1	..	..	..	..	..
Toboggan (?) 68	..	..	..	..	..	..	..	..	..	..	..	..	..
Sledge runner, bone, fragment .... —	..	..	..	..	..	1	..	..	..	..	..	..	..
— small, bone or ivory .... —	..	..	..	..	..	..	..	..	..	..	..	..	..
Sledge shoe, bone 69	..	..	..	..	..	..	..	..	..	..	..	..	1
— ivory .... —	..	..	..	..	..	..	..	..	..	..	..	..	..
— baleen .... —	..	..	..	..	..	..	..	3	1	..	..	..	..
Sledge cross-slat, bone .... —	..	..	2	1	..	..	..	1	..	..	..	..	..
Toggle for draught line 70	..	..	..	..	..	..	..	..	..	..	..	..	..
Trace buckle, egg-shaped .... —	..	..	..	..	..	..	..	..	..	..	2	1	..
— holes at right angles .... —	..	..	..	..	..	..	..	..	..	..	..	..	..
Umiaq cover, fragment .... —	..	..	..	..	..	..	..	..	..	..	..	..	..
Harpoon rest for umiaq (?) 71	..	..	..	..	..	..	..	..	..	..	..	1	..
Boat-hook .... —	..	..	..	..	..	..	1	..	..	..	..	..	..
Kayak deck beam (?), bone .... —	..	..	..	..	..	..	..	..	..	2	..	..	..
End mounting of kayak paddle, broad 72	..	..	..	..	..	..	..	..	..	..	..	..	..
Snow knife:													
Separate handle, wooden with bed for blade 72	..	..	..	..	..	..	..	..	..	..	..	..	..
Separate handle, antler with slit ...... —	..	..	..	..	..	..	..	..	..	..	..	..	..
— blade, walrus ivory .... —	..	..	..	..	..	..	..	..	..	..	..	..	..
Snow probe, bone .... —	..	..	..	..	..	..	..	..	..	..	..	1	..
Snow shovel blade, bone .... —	..	..	..	..	..	..	..	..	..	..	..	..	..
Knife, with end blade (Thule type) .... —	..	..	2	1	..	..	..	1	..	..	..	1	..
— — whittling knife 73	..	..	..	1	..	..	..	1	..	..	..	..	..

III. Archaeological Investigations in the Thule District.

(continued)

	House 18	House 19	House 20	House 21	House 22	House 23	House 24 A	House 24 A+B	House 24 B	House 25	House 26	House 27	House 28	House 29	House 30	House 31	House 32	House 33	House 52	House 54	House 55	House 56	House 57	House 58	House 59	House 60
	..	..	..	..	..	..	..	..	..	..	1	..	..	..	..	..	..	..	..	..	..	..	..	..	..	..
	..	..	..	..	..	..	..	..	..	..	..	..	..	1	..	..	1	..	..	..	..	..	..	..	..	..
	..	..	..	..	..	..	..	..	..	..	4	..	..	..	1	..	..	..	..	..	..	..	..	..	..	..
	..	..	..	..	..	..	..	..	..	..	1	..	..	..	..	1	..	..	..	..	..	..	..	..	..	..
	..	..	..	..	..	..	..	..	..	..	1	..	..	..	..	..	..	..	..	..	..	..	..	..	..	..
	..	..	..	..	..	..	..	..	..	..	..	..	..	..	..	..	1	..	..	..	..	..	..	..	..	..
	1	..	..	..	..	..	..	..	..	..	..	..	..	..	..	..	..	..	..	..	..	..	..	..	..	..
	..	..	..	..	..	..	..	..	..	..	..	..	..	..	..	..	..	..	..	..	..	..	..	..	..	..
	..	..	..	..	..	..	..	..	..	..	..	..	..	1	..	..	..	..	..	..	..	..	..	..	..	..
	..	..	..	2	..	1	1	..	..	..	4	..	1	..	..	..	3	..	..	..	..	..	..	..	..	..
	..	..	..	..	..	..	..	..	..	..	1	..	..	..	..	..	..	..	..	..	..	..	..	..	..	..
	1	..	..	..	..	..	..	..	..	..	..	..	..	..	1	..	1	..	..	..	..	..	..	..	..	..
	..	..	..	..	..	1	..	..	..	..	..	..	..	..	..	..	1	..	..	..	..	..	..	..	..	..
	..	..	..	1	..	..	..	..	..	..	..	..	1	..	..	..	..	..	..	..	..	..	..	..	1	..
	..	..	..	..	..	..	..	..	..	..	..	..	..	..	..	..	..	..	..	..	..	..	..	..	..	..
	..	1	..	..	..	1	..	..	..	..	2	..	..	2	2	1	1	..	..	..	..	..	..	..	..	..
	..	..	2	..	..	..	..	..	..	..	..	..	..	..	..	..	..	..	..	..	..	..	..	..	..	..
	..	..	..	1	..	..	..	..	..	..	1	..	..	..	..	..	1	..	..	..	..	..	..	..	..	..
	..	..	..	..	..	..	..	..	..	..	1	..	..	..	1	..	1	..	..	..	..	..	..	..	..	..
	..	..	1	..	..	1	..	..	..	..	..	..	..	..	3	..	..	..	..	..	..	..	..	..	..	..
	..	..	..	..	..	..	..	..	..	..	..	1	..	..	..	..	..	..	..	..	1	..	..	..	..	..
	..	..	2	..	..	..	..	..	..	..	1	..	..	4	1	..	..	..	..	..	..	..	..	..	..	..
	..	..	1	..	..	..	..	..	..	..	..	..	..	..	..	1	..	..	..	..	..	..	..	1	..	..
	..	..	..	..	..	..	..	..	..	..	..	..	1	..	..	..	..	..	..	..	..	..	..	..	..	..
	..	..	1	..	..	..	..	..	..	..	2	..	1	..	..	..	..	..	..	..	..	..	..	..	..	..
	..	1	..	..	..	..	..	..	..	..	..	..	1	2	..	..	..	..	..	..	..	..	..	..	..	..
	..	..	..	..	..	..	..	..	..	..	..	..	2	..	..	..	..	..	..	..	..	..	..	..	..	..
	..	..	..	..	..	..	..	..	..	..	..	..	..	..	..	..	..	..	..	..	..	..	..	..	..	..
	..	..	..	..	..	1	..	..	..	..	1	..	2	..	..	1	2	..	..	..	..	1	..	..	..	1
	..	..	..	..	..	..	..	..	..	..	..	..	..	..	..	..	..	..	..	..	1	..	..	..	..	..
	..	1	..	..	..	..	..	..	..	..	..	..	..	..	..	..	..	..	..	..	..	..	..	..	..	..
	..	..	..	..	..	..	..	..	1	..	..	..	..	..	..	..	..	..	..	..	..	..	..	..	..	..
	..	..	..	..	..	..	..	..	..	..	1	..	1	..	1	..	..	..	..	..	..	..	..	..	..	..
	..	..	..	..	..	..	..	..	..	..	..	..	..	1	..	..	..	..	..	..	..	..	..	..	..	..
	2	1	2	1	..	2	..	..	..	..	..	1	2	2	3	..	1	..	..	..	..	..	1	..	..	..
	..	1	1	..	..	..	..	..	..	..	..	1	1	..	..	1	..	1	..	..	..	..	..	..	..	..

Table 1

Ref. p.	House 1	House 2	House 3	House 4	House 5	House 6	House 8	House 10	House 11	House 13 A	House 13 B	House 16	House 17
Knife with end blade, handle of two halves 73	..	..	..	..	..	..	..	..	..	..	..	1	..
— — open blade slit —	..	..	..	..	..	..	..	..	..	..	..	..	..
Knife with side blade, wood —	..	..	..	..	..	..	..	..	..	..	..	..	1
Knife blade, iron —	..	..	..	..	1	1	..	1	..	..	..	..	..
Knife of baleen —	..	..	..	..	..	..	..	..	..	..	..	..	..
— —, spatula shaped —	..	..	..	..	..	..	..	..	..	..	..	..	..
Knife of bone —	..	..	..	..	..	..	..	..	..	1	..	..	..
Hand drill —	..	..	..	..	..	..	..	..	..	..	..	..	..
Bow drill shank, bone 74	..	..	..	..	..	..	..	..	..	..	..	..	..
— fore-shaft —	..	..	..	..	..	..	..	..	..	1	..	..	..
— mouthpiece, caribou astragalus —	..	..	..	..	..	..	..	..	..	..	..	..	..
Whetstone —	..	..	..	..	..	1	1	..	..	1	..	2	..
Hammer stone —	..	1	2	..	1	..	..	..	..	1	..	1	1
Flint flaker —	..	..	..	..	..	..	2	2	..	3	1	1	3
Head of a stone maul —	..	..	..	..	..	..	..	..	..	..	..	..	..
Adze head, no holes 75	..	..	..	..	..	..	..	..	..	1	..	..	..
— vertical holes —	..	..	..	..	..	..	..	..	..	..	..	..	..
— horizontal holes —	..	..	..	..	..	..	..	..	..	..	..	..	..
Adze handle, one hole —	..	..	..	..	1	1	..	..	..	..	..	..	..
— 3 holes —	..	..	..	..	..	..	..	..	..	..	..	..	..
Hand pick —	..	..	..	..	1	..	..	..	..	1	..	..	..
Pick-axe head —	..	..	..	..	..	..	..	..	1	..	..	..	..
Mattock blade, bone, bed for handle 76	..	..	..	..	..	..	..	..	..	1	..	..	..
— handle —	..	..	..	..	..	..	..	..	..	..	..	..	..
Hatchet head, ivory or bone 75	..	..	..	..	..	..	..	..	..	..	..	..	..
Chopping-block, whale vertebra 76	..	..	..	..	2	..	..	..	..	..	..	..	1
Wedge —	..	..	..	..	1	..	..	..	..	..	..	..	..
Marline spike, pointed —	..	..	..	..	..	..	..	..	..	..	..	..	..
— flat —	..	..	..	..	..	..	..	..	..	..	..	..	..
Pointed fibula —	..	..	..	..	..	..	..	..	..	..	..	..	..
— ulna —	..	..	..	..	..	..	..	..	..	..	..	..	..
Nail, bone —	..	..	..	..	..	..	1	..	..	..	..	..	..
End scraper, flint, convex edge 77	..	..	..	..	..	..	..	..	..	..	..	..	..
Side scraper, flint, ground edge —	..	..	..	..	..	..	..	..	..	..	..	..	..
Ulo handle, wood 76	..	..	..	..	..	..	..	..	..	..	..	..	..
— — segment-shaped —	..	..	..	..	..	..	..	..	..	..	..	..	..
— bone (trapezoidal) —	..	..	..	..	..	..	..	..	..	..	1	..	..
— — thin with hole —	..	..	..	..	..	..	..	..	..	..	..	..	..
Stone scraper, blunt 77	..	..	..	..	..	..	..	..	..	..	..	..	..
End scraper, narrow, bone —	..	..	..	..	..	..	..	..	..	1	..	..	..
Two-handed scraper, walrus penis-bone —	..	..	..	..	..	..	..	..	1	..	..	..	..
Cup-shaped scraper, ivory 78	..	..	..	..	..	..	..	..	..	..	..	..	..

III Archaeological Investigations in the Thule District. 55

(continued)

House 18	House 19	House 20	House 21	House 22	House 23	House 24 A	House 24 A+B	House 24 B	House 25	House 26	House 27	House 28	House 29	House 30	House 31	House 32	House 33	House 52	House 54	House 55	House 56	House 57	House 58	House 59	House 60
..	..	..	..	..	..	..	..	1	..	..	..	..	..	..	1	..	..	..	..	..	..	..	1	..	..
..	..	..	..	..	..	..	..	..	..	..	..	..	..	1	..	..	..	..	..	..	..	..	..	..	..
..	..	..	..	..	..	..	..	..	..	..	..	..	..	..	..	..	..	..	..	..	..	..	..	..	..
..	..	..	..	1	..	..	1	..	..	..	..	1	..	..	1	..	..	..	..	..	..	..	..	..	..
1	..	..	..	..	..	..	..	..	..	..	1	..	..	..	1	..	..	..	..	..	..	..	..	..	..
..	..	..	..	..	..	..	..	..	..	..	..	..	..	..	1	..	..	..	..	..	..	..	..	..	..
1	..	..	..	..	..	..	..	..	..	..	..	..	..	..	..	..	..	..	..	..	..	..	..	..	..
..	..	..	..	..	..	..	..	..	..	..	..	..	..	1	..	..	..	..	..	..	..	..	..	..	..
1	..	..	..	..	..	..	..	..	..	..	..	..	..	..	..	..	..	..	..	..	..	..	..	..	..
..	..	..	..	..	..	..	..	..	..	..	..	..	..	..	..	..	..	..	..	..	..	..	..	..	..
..	..	..	..	..	..	..	..	1	..	..	..	..	..	..	..	..	..	..	..	..	..	..	..	..	..
..	..	..	1	..	..	1	1	..	1	..	2	..	..	..	..	..	..	..	..	..	..	..	..	..	..
..	1	1	..	..	1	..	..	..	..	3	..	1	..	1	1	3	..	..	..	..	..	..	..	..	..
2	1	2	..	1	..	1	1	..	..	2	..	1	3	1	..	..	..	..	..	..	..	..	..	..	1
2	..	1	..	..	..	..	..	..	..	..	..	..	..	..	..	1	..	..	..	..	..	..	..	1	..
..	..	..	..	..	..	..	..	..	..	..	..	..	..	1	..	..	..	1	..	..	1	..	..	..	..
..	..	..	1	..	..	..	..	..	..	..	..	..	..	..	..	..	..	..	..	..	..	..	..	..	..
..	..	..	..	..	..	..	..	1	..	..	..	..	..	..	1	..	..	..	..	..	..	..	..	..	..
..	..	..	..	..	..	..	..	..	..	..	..	1	..	..	..	..	..	..	..	..	..	..	..	..	..
..	..	..	1	..	..	..	..	..	..	..	..	..	..	1	..	..	..	..	..	..	..	..	..	..	..
1	..	..	..	..	1	..	..	..	..	1	..	..	..	1	..	..	..	..	..	..	..	..	..	..	..
..	..	..	..	..	..	..	..	..	..	..	..	..	..	..	..	1	..	..	..	..	..	..	..	..	..
..	..	..	..	..	..	..	1	..	1	..	..	..	..	..	..	..	..	..	..	..	..	1	..	..	..
..	..	..	..	..	..	..	..	..	..	..	..	1	..	..	..	1	..	..	..	..	..	..	..	..	..
1	..	..	..	..	..	1	..	..	..	..	..	..	..	..	..	..	..	..	..	..	..	..	..	..	..
..	..	1	..	..	..	..	..	..	..	..	..	..	..	1	..	1	..	..	..	..	..	1	..	..	..
2	..	..	..	..	..	..	..	..	..	1	..	1	..	..	..	4	1	..	..	..	..	1	..	..	..
..	..	1	1	..	..	..	..	..	..	..	..	..	..	1	..	..	..	..	..	..	..	..	..	..	..
..	1	..	..	..	..	..	..	..	..	..	..	..	..	..	..	..	..	..	..	..	..	..	..	..	..
..	..	..	..	..	..	..	..	..	..	..	..	..	..	..	..	..	..	..	..	1	..	..	..	..	..
..	..	..	..	1	..	..	..	..	..	..	..	..	..	..	..	..	..	..	..	..	..	..	..	..	..
..	..	..	..	..	1	..	..	..	..	..	1	..	1	..	1	..	..	..	..	..	..	..	..	..	..
..	..	..	..	..	..	..	..	1	..	..	..	..	..	..	..	..	..	..	..	..	..	..	..	..	..
..	..	..	..	..	..	..	..	..	1	..	..	..	..	..	..	..	..	..	..	..	..	..	..	..	..
..	..	..	1	..	..	..	..	..	..	..	..	..	..	..	..	..	..	..	..	..	..	..	..	..	..
..	..	..	..	..	..	..	..	..	1	..	..	..	..	..	..	..	..	..	..	..	..	..	..	..	..
..	..	..	..	..	..	..	..	..	..	..	..	..	..	..	..	..	1	..	..	..	..	..	..	..	..
..	..	..	..	..	1	..	..	..	..	..	..	..	1	..	..	1	..	..	..	..	..	..	..	..	..
..	..	..	..	..	..	..	1	..	..	..	..	..	..	..	..	..	..	..	..	..	..	..	..	..	..
..	2	2	..	..	..	..	..	..	1	..	..	..	1	..	..	..	..	..	..	..	..	..	..	..	..
..	..	..	..	..	..	..	..	..	..	..	2	..	..	..	..	..	..	..	..	..	..	..	..	..	..
..	..	..	..	..	..	..	..	..	..	..	..	2	..	..	..	..	..	..	..	..	..	..	..	..	..

Table 1

	Ref. p.	House 1	House 2	House 3	House 4	House 5	House 6	House 8	House 10	House 11	House 13 A	House 13 B	House 16	House 17
Fat scraper, bone with straight edge	78	..	..	..	..	..	..	..	..	..	..	..	..	..
Urine scraper, ivory	—	..	..	..	..	..	..	..	..	..	1	..	..	..
Bodkin	—	..	..	..	..	..	..	..	..	..	..	..	..	..
Needle, bone	—	..	..	..	..	..	..	..	..	..	..	..	..	..
Thimble	—	..	..	..	..	..	..	..	2	..	..	..	..	..
Pyrite	—	1	1	1	..	1	5	..	3	..	1	2	1	..
Lamp of soapstone, no ledge, fragment	—	..	..	..	1	..	..	..	..	..	1	..	..	..
Lamp trimmer, wood	79	1	..	..	1	1	..	1	1	1	3	2	..	1
Cooking pot, soapstone, fragment	—	..	2	..	2	1	..	..	1	1	1	2	3	..
Lamp (and pot) of clay	—	..	..	..	..	..	..	..	..	..	..	..	..	..
Meat tray, wood	—	..	..	..	..	..	1	..	..	..	..	..	..	..
Oval bowl, side of baleen	80	..	..	..	..	..	..	1	1	..	1	1	..	..
— bottom, bone	—	..	..	..	..	..	..	..	..	..	..	..	1	1
— — baleen	—	..	..	..	..	..	..	1	..	..	..	..	..	..
Ladle, wood	—	..	..	..	..	..	..	..	..	..	..	..	..	..
— musk-ox horn	—	..	..	..	..	..	..	..	..	..	..	..	..	..
Meat stick, bone	—	..	..	..	..	..	..	..	..	..	..	..	..	1
Blubber fork	—	..	..	..	..	..	..	..	..	..	..	..	..	3
Fish spoon (?), baleen	—	..	..	..	..	..	..	..	..	..	..	..	..	..
Baleen handle	—	..	..	..	..	..	..	..	..	..	1	..	..	..
Pot hook	—	..	..	..	..	..	..	..	..	..	..	1	..	..
Carrying stick (?), baleen	—	..	..	..	..	..	..	..	..	..	..	..	..	..
Edge mounting, bone	—	..	..	..	..	..	..	..	..	..	..	..	..	..
Gutskin jacket	81	..	..	..	..	..	..	..	..	..	..	..	..	..
Birdskin jacket	86	..	..	..	..	..	..	..	..	..	..	..	..	..
Loose hood of birdskin	—	..	..	..	..	..	..	..	..	..	..	..	..	..
Birdskin trousers	—	..	..	..	..	..	..	..	..	..	..	..	..	..
Boot top	87	..	..	..	..	..	..	..	..	..	..	..	..	..
— sole	88	..	..	..	..	..	..	..	1	..	..	..	..	..
Stocking	—	..	..	..	..	..	..	..	..	..	..	..	..	..
Baleen wool	89	..	..	..	1	..	1	1	1	..	..	..	..	..
Mittens	—	..	..	..	..	..	..	..	1	..	..	..	..	..
Button, toggle-shaped, seal phalanx	90	..	..	..	..	..	..	..	..	..	..	..	..	..
— —	—	..	..	..	..	..	..	..	..	..	..	1	..	..
— ventral hole	—	..	..	..	..	..	..	..	..	..	..	4	..	..
Buckle, flat with two holes	—	..	..	..	..	..	1	..	..	..	..	..	..	..
— tube-shaped	—	..	..	..	..	..	..	..	..	..	..	..	..	..
Tooth pendant	—	..	..	..	..	..	..	..	..	..	..	..	..	..
— bear tooth	—	..	1	..	..	..	..	..	1	..	..	..	..	..
Pendant, soapstone	—	..	..	..	..	..	..	..	..	..	..	..	1	..
— ivory	—	..	..	..	..	..	..	..	..	..	..	..	..	..

III Archaeological Investigations in the Thule District. 57

(continued)

	House 18	House 19	House 20	House 21	House 22	House 23	House 24 A	House 24 A+B	House 24 B	House 25	House 26	House 27	House 28	House 29	House 30	House 31	House 32	House 33	House 52	House 54	House 55	House 56	House 57	House 58	House 59	House 60
	..	..	..	..	..	..	..	..	..	..	..	1	..	..	..	..	..	..	..	..	..	..	..	..	..	..
	..	..	..	..	..	..	..	..	..	..	..	..	..	..	..	..	..	..	..	..	..	..	..	..	..	..
	..	..	..	..	..	..	..	..	..	..	1	..	..	..	..	..	..	..	..	..	..	..	..	..	..	..
	..	..	..	..	..	..	..	..	..	..	..	1	..	..	..	..	..	..	..	..	..	..	..	..	..	..
	..	..	..	..	..	..	..	..	..	..	1	..	..	..	..	..	..	..	..	..	..	..	..	..	..	..
	2	..	..	4	2	2	1	1	5	7	11	3	1	3	..	1	3	..	..	1	1	..	1	..	..	..
	..	..	..	..	..	..	..	..	..	..	1	..	..	..	1	..	..	..	..	..	..	..	..	..	..	..
	..	2	2	..	1	3	4	2	..	..	2	1	1	1	3	..	..	..	..	..	1	..	2	1	..	..
	2	1	..	1	1	18	2	2	1	..	2	..	3	3	7	13	1	1	..	..	..	..	..	..	..	..
	..	..	..	..	..	..	..	..	..	..	..	..	..	..	..	..	2	..	..	..	..	..	..	..	..	..
	..	..	..	..	..	..	..	..	..	..	..	1	..	..	..	..	2	..	..	..	..	..	..	..	..	..
	..	..	..	..	..	..	..	..	..	..	..	..	..	1	..	..	..	..	..	..	..	..	..	..	..	..
	..	..	..	..	..	..	..	..	..	..	..	..	..	..	..	1	..	..	..	..	..	..	..	..	..	..
	..	..	..	..	..	..	..	..	..	..	..	..	..	1	..	..	..	..	..	..	..	..	..	..	..	..
	..	..	..	..	1	..	..	..	..	..	..	..	..	..	..	..	..	..	..	..	..	..	..	..	..	..
	..	..	..	..	..	..	..	..	..	..	..	..	..	1	..	..	..	..	..	..	..	..	..	..	..	..
	..	..	..	..	..	..	..	..	..	..	..	..	..	1	..	..	..	..	..	..	1	..	..	..	1	..
	1	..	..	..	..	..	..	..	..	..	..	1	..	..	..	..	..	..	..	..	..	..	..	..	..	..
	..	..	..	..	..	..	..	..	..	..	1	..	..	..	..	..	..	..	..	..	..	..	..	..	..	..
	..	..	..	..	..	..	..	..	..	..	..	..	..	..	..	1	..	..	..	..	..	..	..	..	..	..
	..	..	..	..	..	..	..	..	..	..	..	..	..	..	..	..	..	..	..	..	..	..	..	..	..	..
	..	..	..	..	..	..	..	..	..	..	1	..	..	..	..	..	..	..	..	..	..	..	..	..	..	..
	1	..	..	..	..	..	..	..	..	..	..	..	..	..	..	..	..	..	..	..	..	..	..	..	..	..
	..	..	..	..	1	..	..	..	..	..	..	..	3	..	..	..	..	..	..	..	..	..	..	..	..	..
	..	..	..	..	..	..	..	..	..	..	..	..	1	..	..	..	..	..	..	..	..	..	..	..	..	..
	..	..	..	..	..	..	..	..	..	..	..	..	1	..	..	..	..	..	..	..	..	..	..	..	..	..
	..	..	..	..	..	..	..	..	..	..	..	..	1	..	..	..	..	..	..	..	..	..	..	..	..	..
	..	..	..	..	..	..	..	..	..	..	..	..	2	..	..	..	..	..	..	..	..	..	..	..	..	..
	..	..	..	..	1	..	..	..	..	..	1	..	..	1	..	..	..	..	..	..	..	..	..	..	..	..
	..	..	..	..	..	..	..	..	..	..	1	..	..	..	..	..	..	..	..	..	..	..	..	..	..	..
	..	..	1	..	..	..	..	..	..	..	1	..	..	1	..	..	..	..	..	..	..	..	..	..	..	..
	..	..	..	..	..	..	..	..	..	..	2	..	..	..	..	..	..	..	..	..	..	..	..	..	..	..
	..	..	..	..	1	..	..	..	..	..	..	..	..	..	..	..	..	..	..	..	..	..	..	..	..	..
	..	..	..	..	..	..	..	..	..	..	..	..	..	..	..	..	..	..	..	..	..	..	..	..	..	..
	..	..	..	..	..	..	..	..	..	..	..	..	1	..	..	..	..	..	..	..	..	..	..	..	..	..
	..	..	..	..	..	..	..	..	..	..	..	..	..	..	..	..	..	..	..	..	..	..	..	..	..	..
	..	..	..	..	..	1	..	..	..	..	1	..	..	..	..	..	..	..	..	..	..	..	..	..	..	..
	..	..	72	..	..	..	..	..	..	..	1	..	..	..	..	2	..	..	..	..	..	..	..	..	..	..
	..	..	1	..	1	..	..	..	..	..	..	..	2	1	..	..	..	..	..	..	..	..	1	1	..	..
	..	..	..	..	..	..	..	..	..	..	..	..	..	..	..	..	..	..	..	..	..	..	..	..	..	..
	..	..	1	..	..	..	..	..	..	..	..	..	1	..	..	..	1	..	..	..	..	..	..	..	..	..

Table 1

	Ref. p.	House 1	House 2	House 3	House 4	House 5	House 6	House 8	House 10	House 11	House 13 A	House 13 B	House 16	House 17
Pendant, chain	91	..	..	..	..	..	..	..	..	..	..	..	..	..
Bead, amber	90													
Snow beater, baleen	91	..	..	..	3	..	..	2	1	..	..	..	..	1
Fragments of skin	—	..	..	..	..	..	..	1	2	..	4	1	1	2
— seal thong	—	..	..	..	..	..	..	..	1	..	..	..	..	..
Plaited sinew thread	—	..	..	..	..	..	..	..	..	..	..	..	..	1
Ajagaq, seal humerus	—	..	..	..	..	..	..	..	..	..	..	..	..	..
— stick	—	..	1	..	..	..	..	..	..	..	..	..	..	..
Gambling bone	—	..	..	..	..	..	..	2	..	..	1	1	..	..
Top-disk, baleen	—	..	..	..	1	..	..	..	..	..	..	..	..	..
Bear figure	—	..	..	..	..	..	..	..	..	..	..	1	..	..
Dog figure	—	..	..	..	..	..	..	..	..	..	..	1	..	..
"Swimming bird"	—	..	..	..	..	..	..	..	..	..	..	..	..	..
Doll, wood	—	..	..	..	..	..	..	..	1	..	..	..	..	..
Bird bones, put one into another	—	..	..	..	..	..	..	..	..	..	..	..	..	..
"Dart" of bird quill	—	..	..	..	..	..	..	..	..	..	..	..	..	..
Toy harpoon, wood	—	..	..	..	..	..	..	..	..	..	..	..	..	..
— dart (or leister), baleen	92	..	..	..	..	..	..	..	..	..	..	..	..	..
— bow, wood	—	..	..	..	..	..	..	..	..	..	..	..	..	..
— arrow, wood	—	..	..	..	..	..	..	..	..	..	..	..	..	..
— — baleen	—	..	..	..	..	..	..	..	..	..	..	..	..	1
— — shaft, butt	—	..	..	..	..	..	..	..	..	..	..	..	..	..
— sling handle, wood	—	..	..	..	..	..	..	..	..	..	..	..	..	..
— sledge, cross bar, wood	—	..	..	..	..	..	..	..	..	..	..	..	..	..
— umiaq, wood	—	..	..	..	..	..	..	..	..	..	..	..	..	..
— — oar blade	—	..	..	..	..	..	..	..	..	..	..	..	..	..
— kayak	—	..	..	..	..	..	..	..	..	..	..	..	..	..
— snow knife with handle hole	—	..	..	..	..	..	..	..	..	..	..	..	..	1
— lamp	—	..	..	..	..	..	..	..	..	..	..	..	..	..
— cooking pot	—	..	..	..	..	..	..	..	..	..	..	..	..	..
Drum, baleen	—	..	..	..	..	..	..	..	..	..	..	1	..	..
— handle, wood	—	..	..	..	..	..	..	..	..	..	..	1	..	..
Amulet bundle	93	..	..	..	..	..	..	..	..	..	..	..	..	..
— box, wood	—	..	..	..	..	..	..	..	..	..	..	..	..	..
Unidentifiable pieces of worked bone etc.	—	..	..	1	4	1	3	2	6	2	10	6	9	4
— — wood	—	1	4	1	..	1	5	3	1	1	7	5	..	2
— — baleen	94	..	..	..	..	..	..	2	3	..	3	2	3	3
Baleen strips	—	..	..	..	1	..	..	2	..	..	..	..	..	1
— line with knots	—	1	..	1	3	..	1	2	2	1	1	2	1	2
Waste flint	95	..	..	..	..	..	..	..	..	..	..	1	..	..
Mica	—	..	..	..	1	1	..	..	..	..	..	..	..	..
Iron	—	..	..	..	..	..	..	..	1	..	2	1	..	..

III Archaeological Investigations in the Thule District.

(continued)

	House 18	House 19	House 20	House 21	House 22	House 23	House 24 A	House 24 A+B	House 24 B	House 25	House 26	House 27	House 28	House 29	House 30	House 31	House 32	House 33	House 52	House 54	House 55	House 56	House 57	House 58	House 59	House 60
	..	..	..	..	..	..	..	..	..	..	2	..	..	..	..	..	..	..	..	..	..	..	..	..	..	..
	..	..	..	..	..	..	..	..	..	..	..	..	..	..	..	..	..	..	..	..	..	..	1	..	..	..
	..	1	..	..	..	..	..	..	..	..	..	..	..	..	..	1	..	..	..	..	..	..	..	..	..	..
	..	..	1	..	..	1	..	..	..	..	4	..	1	..	..	..	..	..	..	..	..	..	..	..	..	..
	..	..	..	..	..	..	..	..	..	..	2	..	..	1	1	..	..	..	..	..	..	..	..	..	..	..
	..	..	..	..	..	..	..	..	..	..	..	..	1	..	..	..	..	..	..	..	..	..	..	..	..	..
	..	..	1	..	..	..	..	..	..	..	..	..	..	..	..	..	..	..	..	..	..	..	..	..	..	..
	..	..	..	..	..	..	..	..	..	..	..	..	..	..	..	..	..	..	..	..	..	..	..	..	..	..
	1	..	3	..	..	1	..	..	..	..	..	..	2	..	1	..	1	..	..	..	..	1	..	1	..	..
	..	..	..	..	..	..	..	..	..	..	..	..	..	1	..	..	..	..	..	..	..	..	..	..	..	..
	..	..	..	..	..	..	..	1	..	..	..	..	..	..	..	1	..	..	..	..	..	..	..	..	..	..
	..	..	..	..	..	..	..	..	..	..	..	..	..	..	..	..	1	..	..	..	..	..	..	..	..	..
	..	..	..	..	..	..	..	..	..	..	..	..	..	..	..	..	..	1	..	..	..	..	..	..	..	..
	..	..	..	..	..	..	..	..	..	..	2	..	..	..	..	..	..	..	..	..	..	..	..	..	..	..
	..	..	..	1	..	..	..	..	..	..	..	..	..	..	..	1	..	..	..	..	..	..	1	..	..	..
	..	..	..	..	..	..	..	..	..	..	..	..	..	1	..	..	..	..	..	..	..	..	..	..	..	..
	..	..	..	..	..	..	..	..	..	..	1	..	..	..	..	..	..	..	..	..	..	..	..	..	..	..
	..	..	..	..	..	..	..	..	..	..	..	..	..	1	1	..	..	..	..	..	..	..	..	..	..	..
	..	..	..	..	..	..	..	..	..	..	1	..	..	..	..	..	..	..	..	..	..	..	..	..	..	..
	..	..	..	..	..	..	..	..	..	..	2	..	..	..	..	..	..	..	..	..	..	..	..	..	..	..
	..	..	..	..	..	..	..	..	..	..	3	..	..	..	..	..	..	..	..	..	..	..	..	..	..	..
	..	..	..	1	..	..	..	..	..	..	..	..	..	..	..	..	..	..	..	..	..	..	..	..	..	..
	..	..	..	..	..	..	..	..	..	..	..	..	..	..	..	..	1	..	..	..	..	..	..	..	..	..
	..	..	..	..	..	..	..	..	..	..	..	..	..	1	..	..	..	..	..	..	..	..	..	..	..	..
	..	..	..	..	..	..	..	..	..	..	1	..	..	..	..	..	..	..	..	..	..	..	..	..	..	..
	..	..	..	..	..	1	..	..	..	..	..	..	..	..	..	..	..	..	..	..	..	..	..	..	..	..
	..	..	..	..	..	..	..	..	..	..	..	..	..	..	..	..	..	..	..	..	..	..	..	..	..	..
	..	..	..	..	..	..	..	..	..	1	..	..	..	..	1	..	..	..	..	..	..	..	..	..	1	..
	..	..	1	1	..	1	..	..	..	..	..	..	..	..	..	..	..	..	..	..	..	..	..	..	..	..
	..	..	..	..	..	..	..	..	..	..	..	..	..	..	..	..	..	..	..	..	..	..	..	..	..	..
	..	..	1	..	..	..	..	..	..	..	..	..	..	..	..	..	..	..	..	..	..	..	..	..	..	..
	..	..	..	..	..	..	..	..	..	..	..	..	..	..	..	1	..	..	..	..	..	..	..	..	..	..
	..	1	6	2	4	6	7	8	14	4	9	2	11	4	13	5	13	5	6	1	1	3	2	5	1	..
	2	6	1	2	2	3	3	1	5	1	11	..	12	5	5	..	5	..	..	..	..	..	..	..	..	..
	1	..	4	..	..	..	3	..	1	1	4	1	2	4	2	1	1	..	..	..	..	..	..	..	1	..
	..	..	..	..	..	..	..	..	..	..	..	..	..	..	2	..	..	..	..	..	..	..	..	..	..	..
	1	..	1	1	1	1	1	..	1	..	2	1	2	1	2	1	1	1	..	..	..	..	..	..	..	..
	..	..	1	..	..	..	..	..	1	..	1	..	..	..	..	..	1	..	..	..	..	..	..	..	..	..
	..	..	..	..	1	..	..	..	..	..	..	..	..	..	..	..	..	..	..	..	..	..	..	..	..	..
	..	..	2	..	1	2	1	..	2	1	2	..	3	..	1	1	2	1	..	..	..	..	..	..	..	..

Ruin 60, (plan fig. 34), lies west of ruin 55 and 59. The front part of the floor forms a narrow depression, about 0.5 × 1.7 m, across the longitudinal direction of the ruin, and about 45 cm below the surface outside. At the sides were remains of a stone skirting, and the bottom was partly paved. A larger flag lay at the east end, where the entrance had been. From this front part a narrow passage leads in, sloping up

Fig. 37. Tent-ring near house 6, Nûgdlît.

towards the inner part, which again forms an oval depression. As in the other ruins of this type the gravel benches at the sides were laid with small, flat stones. On the front part of the floor lay some bones, pieces of baleen, etc. — Finds: L3:13221—13223.

Small depressions like those described above were found in many places, indicated on the plan in fig. 3 by stippled circles, but time did not allow us to make a closer investigation.

Between the house ruins some *tent-rings* were found, the age of which could not be determined. The tent-ring shown in fig. 37, lying immediately to the east of house 6, seems to be very old. Another one is seen on the plan in fig. 26. It lies close to ruin 52. Both of them have an extension of about $3^1/_2 \times 4$ m. The latter has a peculiar arrangement of large stones in the middle, as if they formed a kind of lamp stand, or the like, in front of the platform.

Description of the objects found.

Just as the whole group of ruins excavated suggests that they belong to a rather narrowly limited period of habitation, so the finds suggest the same thing. Compared with the material described in part I they reveal an obvious poverty in types which is remarkable when the number of specimens found is taken into consideration. It is therefore thought reasonable to describe the objects collectively.

Harpoon heads.

A total of 37 harpoon heads was found, including fragments identifiable as to type. All are of the toggle type. Thirty one are made of walrus ivory, 4 of antler and 2 of bone. Of these, 36 specimens belong to three main types: Thule-2, Thule-3, both with open shaft-socket, and the type with a closed socket and strong dorsal spur (cf. I. Pl. 4.9-11, 18). Finally, a fragment of a harpoon head of Inugsuk type was found.

The harpoon heads with an open socket all have slots for the lashing, and the bottom of the socket is made by a vertical cut. On a few specimens, both of type Thule-2 and Thule-3, a tendency to make the socket undercut can be seen.

Thule-2 type. — Fourteen specimens, including fragments. Two are of the simple Thule-2 type. On one of these, L3:12967, one of the barbs is broken, but a new barb had been cut further forward; length 14.3 cm. On L3:12689 the point had been damaged and had been cut into a "human-like" shape. Four fore-ends, broken at the barbs were found. An unfinished specimen and four fragments of butts also belong, as far as can be seen, to the Thule-2 type.

Two specimens have an elongated triangular face on both sides with cross-etchings pointing forwards from the linehole (Pl. 1.5-6). On L3:12637 the ornament ends in a figure V. L3:12900 has a small knob (rudimentary spur) at the root of the spur. A similar knob can be seen on an unornamented specimen, L3:12302 (Pl. 1.4). All are made of walrus ivory, except the unfinished specimen mentioned above.

Thule-3 type. — 14 specimens of which 10 are almost complete, one unfinished, and three fragments. Two are of antler, two of bone, the rest of walrus ivory. All belong more or less distinctly to the type with a hexagonal cross-section in front (cf. I. Pl. 4.5-6). Their lengths vary from 14.1 to 7.5 cm. Only three specimens, shown on Pl. 1.1-3, differ from the others, partly in having a knob on the spur; partly in the characteristic shape of the fore-end, similar to that in I. Pl. 3.14, which gives them a certain Punuk-like character. L3:12196, from house

13. A, is an extremely fine specimen with ornamentations on all four sides. The three sides not seen on Pl. 1.1 are shown in fig. 38.A. The fragment shown on Pl. 1.14 is of a fore-end of a harpoon head of a more slender type, split at the blade slit. It was found in ruin 57. On each side of the sharp keel there is an oblong ornament consisting of two lines with alternating spurs on their inner sides, and converging ends (fig. 38.B). In front, an 'eye' has been etched on both sides, giving to the whole a conventionalized animal-like form. L3:12901, from house

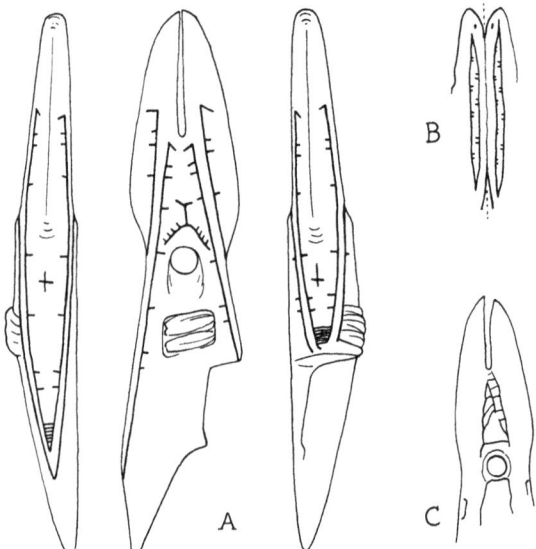

Fig. 38. Ornamented harpoon heads from Nûgdlît, (A) L3:12196, (B) L3:13184, (C) L3:12901. 1:2.

29, seen on Pl. 1.2 and in fig. 38.C, has a cursorily etched line ornament on the side with the socket.—Two strong, broken spurs are of a shape which probably places them in the category Thule-3. On one of them, L3:12968 from house 30, a small knob may be seen at the root.

Harpoon heads with closed socket. — Oblique spur. — L3:12638 from house 24.B is in all respects similar to the above mentioned harpoon heads of the Thule-3 type, except that the shaft-socket is closed. It is made of walrus ivory, of slender form, 11.5 cm long, the fore part hexagonal, with its greatest height a little in front of the line-hole. The socket is broken.

Single, dorsal spur; blade parallel to the line-hole. — Three specimens, all of walrus ivory. L3:12058 from house 4, 8.3 cm long, is almost like that in I. Pl. 4.10. L3:12577 from house 24.A-B is a fragment of a harpoon head about 11.5 cm long, with a more rounded cross-section and a 3.5 cm long blade slit. L3:12823 is a fragment of a strong harpoon head with hexagonal cross-section. L3:12824 is a broken butt.

Inugsuk type. — L3:12520 from house 22 is a much weathered butt of an Inugsuk harpoon head of walrus ivory with two symmetrical, dorsal spurs (cf. I. Pl. 4.19).

Other parts of the harpoon. — Lance.

Swivel. — A fine specimen of walrus ivory, L3:12905, seen Pl. 1.9, was found in house 29. It is barrel-shaped, 4.5 cm long, max. diam. 2 cm, with three 'windows', and with an ornamental spur-line at each end. The spindle is made of antler, 3 cm long, with an oblong hole.

Stoppers for harpoon line. — Four specimens, three of them of walrus ivory, one of antler, lengths 4—5.8 cm. Three have the spike at the end, as shown on Pl. 1.15. On L3:12690 from house 26 the spike is placed almost in the middle (cf. I. Pl. 5.12).

Mouthpieces for harpoon bladder. — Four specimens, all of walrus ivory. Three are of the flat, oval form with a deep groove, as in I. Pl. 5.16; length 2.9—3.3 cm. L3:12059 is smaller, like that in I. Pl. 5.17.

Plugs for mouthpiece. — Five specimens of wood, as in I. Pl. 5.20; length 5.3—7.7 cm. L3:12666 is made from the butt of an arrow shaft.

Bone toggle for harpoon bladder. — One specimen of bone, L3:12102, of the type shown in I. Pl. 5.33, but of a more irregular shape. The length is 9.8 cm.

Mending plugs for bladder. — Pl. 1.11 is a small plug of walrus ivory with a deep groove. The extension at the end has the shape of a curious animal head with a flat 'face' with a small concavity, and a bipartite lower part. The length is 2.2 cm.

Movable foreshafts. — Only one almost complete specimen was found, L3:12197. It is now 18.1 cm long, but appears to have been a little longer. It is of walrus ivory, with one hole, like that in I. Pl. 6.18, but the butt is less pointed. At the fore-end a piece has been flaked off, making a convenient rest for the thumb, the specimen no doubt having been used as a flint flaker.—Four butts of foreshafts, broken at the hole, are more pointed. Two of these are of walrus ivory, two of bone. On one of them, L3:13159, the end has later been roughly flattened; it is rounded by wear and seems to have been used as a narrow scraper for skin softening. — No ice-harpoon foreshafts were found.

Socket pieces. — Six specimens have the butt with a scarf, as in I. Pl. 6.2, most of them with two plug holes, and with the surface of the wedge-shaped part roughened. Four fragments of fore-ends apparently belong to the same type. Three of the specimens are of walrus ivory, two of narwhal tusk, four of bone, and one of antler. In two of the specimens, L3:12118 and 13013, the fore part has a hole right through, as in I. Pl. 6.2,4. Eight of the socket pieces are of the heavy type, and two, L3:12826 and 12902, of the more slender type; with diameters, at the fore-end, of about 2 and 1.5 cm. L3:12826 is of bone, rather roughly made, with a socket 1.2 cm wide and 2 cm deep, in the fore end. L3:12902, from house 29, is shown on Pl. 1.24. It is of walrus ivory, tapering a little towards the fore-end where it has a roughened belt for a lashing, a piece having been split off. The socket is very narrow, only 0.55 cm in diameter and 1.5 cm deep. — Possibly these small socket pieces belonged to bladder darts.

L3:12903, from house 29, is a fragment split off a *cylindrical socket piece* of bone, 8 cm long. At the fore-end it has a deep groove for a lashing. Near the butt end is a small, oblong hole, also for repair.

Ice picks. — Nine identifiable specimens, all belonging to the type with a more or less pyramidal butt (cf. I. Pl. 7.5-6). Seven are of walrus ivory, two of bone. Only L3:12694, made of a walrus tusk is complete. Near the butt is a hole, as in I. Pl. 7.8. L3:12060 is more slender and made of bone. The others are broken butts. — Three broken fore-ends of ice picks are of walrus ivory, narwhal tusk and bone respectively.

Movable lance heads. — Five specimens, none of which are complete. On three of them the fore end is broken; the butt is conical with the end rounded, like that in I. Pl. 7.2. L3:12382, which is made of narwhal tusk, has two holes in the butt and a hole at the fracture. L3:12198 has three holes in the butt, one behind the other. The latter specimen has the fore-end flattened, apparently for use as a scraper; its length is 27.4 cm. L3:13075 is of bone, with a flat rhombic cross-section, 3.2×1.6 cm in the middle. In the butt, close to the conical end, are two holes one close behind the other. On one side is a longitudinal groove leading towards the fore-end, as in I. Pl. 7.2. — Two broken fore-ends of walrus ivory are similar to that shown in I. Pl. 7.1, having a sharply defined, sunken belt for a lashing at the fore-end; one is 3 cm, the other 2.3 cm broad. On the opposite side is a plane bed for a blade. On each of the specimens the fore-end of a longitudinal groove can be seen, ending 5.5 and 3.2 cm respectively from the end of the lance head.

Accessories for kayak- and ice-hunting.

Plugs for towing bladder (?). — Two solid plugs of walrus ivory having an oval cross-section, a deep groove for a lashing, and a hole for a line. One is seen on Pl. 1.21. L3:12582 is similar only smaller: 2.2 cm long. Presumably such plugs belong to towing bladders.

Wound pins. — Three specimens of the type shown in I. Pl. 9.3-6 are all of walrus ivory, length 10.4—11.2 cm. Two of them were found inserted in a strip of hairy sealskin. — Three broken points are probably also from wound pins.

Sealing stool legs. — L3:12521, length 12.7 cm, and L3:12937, length 15.7 cm, are of wood with the characteristic, obliquely cut off, upper end.

Fig. 39. Line buckle of bear shape, from Nûgdlît house 13.B.

Drag line handles of wood. — L3:12988 is round, tapering a little towards the ends, 9.2 cm long and 1.7 cm in diam. in the middle, where it has a groove, as shown in I. Pl. 8.16. L3:12717 is heavier, 15.2 cm long, and narrower in the middle, as in I. Pl. 8.12. — Two small, toggle-shaped handles of wood 7.5 cm long, L3:12306 and 12566, have a flat projection at both ends, as in I. Pl. 8.17.

Line buckles. — L3:12733, from house 26, shown on Pl. 1.18, is a handsome specimen of walrus ivory, carved in the shape of a bear's head, similar to I. Pl. 38.5. In the broad end part there is a rather wide, round hole, and beneath it an oblong slot. Just in front of the round hole are two parallel, ornamental lines with spurs pointing forwards, and, on the upper side, a line with spurs on both sides runs forwards, ending in a V. The bear's head is very delicately modelled.

Another buckle, L3:12276, is seen on Pl. 1.19. It has the shape of a whole bear. The fore and hind legs respectively have not been separated below, thus forming the sides of an oval hole, as shown on fig. 39.

Toggle with oblong hole. — L3:12258 is a small toggle of walrus ivory, like that in I. Pl. 16.8.

Other hunting implements.

Mouth piece for bladder-dart bladder. — L3:12693 is a mouth piece of walrus ivory with a flat under side, like that in I. Pl. 5.14, length 3.2 cm.

Side prong of bird dart. — Two specimens of walrus ivory, each with one barb on the outer, and two on the inner side. The butt has a sharp, convex edge on the inner side, and in front of this is a roughened belt; cf. I. Pl. 10.2.

Weapon shafts. — 13 fragments of wooden shafts were found, most of them with a scarf; diams. 1.5—4.2 cm.

Bow of wood. — L3:12147 is a 5 cm long piece of a wooden bow stave, 2.7 × 1.5 cm in cross-section. On the inner side traces of cross etching can be seen.

Bows of baleen. — Two complete baleen bows were found, in addition to two broken ends. To judge from their size they can only have been destined for children. L3:12884 is 54.3 cm long, its breadth being 2.6 cm in the middle, decreasing towards the ends. L3:12728 is 27.5 cm long and a little narrower in the middle. The cross-section is trapezoidal in the middle, and more triangular towards the ends, the bow having sharp edges on the outer side, the inner side being more rounded. — L3:12739, from house 26, is a 7 cm long end piece of a bow with reflex ends (cf. I. Pl. 47.8).

Bow braces. — L3:12494 is most likely a bow brace of bone, rectangular in shape, 6.2 cm long × 2.3 cm broad, and 0.7 cm thick in the middle. The convex side has two shallow, longitudinal grooves, presumably for the sinew backing. L3:12790, which somewhat resembles that shown in I. Pl. 10.23, is made of baleen, curved, and flattened towards the rounded ends. Its length is 10.5 cm, breadth 1.3 cm.

Sinew twisters. — L3:12907, from house 29, shown on Pl. 1.23, is a fine specimen of walrus ivory with an elongated triangular hole. A broken piece, L3:13078, is also made of walrus ivory.

Arrow heads. — On all arrow heads with the tang preserved the tang has a raised ridge in the middle. No tangs with small knobs, such as are characteristic of the eastern Thule culture, were found. — Six of the arrow heads have a *round, slender point*. Three of these are of walrus ivory, three of antler, of lengths 9—15.5 cm, and diams. 0.3 —0.9 cm (cf. I. Pl. 11.1). The thinnest one, L3:12704, no doubt belongs to a child's arrow. — Two specimens have *unsymmetrical lanceolate* blades, similar to that in I. Pl. 11.8, but longer. Of these L3:12700 is of walrus ivory, L3:13046 of antler. — On L3:12699, which is made of walrus ivory, the blade is widened on one side, forming a barb, in the rear as in I. Pl. 11.25, except that the blade is only 5.5 cm long. — A fragment of an arrow head of walrus ivory, L3:13045, broken at the rearmost barb, is of the type with *more than one barb on one side*, as seen in I. Pl. 12.1. — L3:12383, made of walrus ivory, and 12.6 cm long, is round, with an *egg-shaped fore-end* like that in I. Pl. 11.20, but without a blade slit. Possibly it had not been finished. — L3:12906, seen on Pl. 1.25, made of walrus ivory, has a *bed for a separate blade* and a sunken belt for the lashing. — L3:12255, Pl. 1.26, is also of walrus ivory. It has a sharp *barb on one side*, and on the opposite side, towards the fore-end it has a sharp edge. The fore-end is *egg-shaped, with a blade slit*, one half of it now being split off. — A split-off fragment of a fore-end, L3:13009, also seems to have had a blade slit.

Arrow shafts. — Of five butts of wooden arrow shafts, three are like those shown in I. Pl. 12.7-8, two are wider, like that in I. Pl. 41.26. — Of 11 fragments of arrow shafts eight have a circular, three a flat, oval, cross-section. Eight of the specimens have a scarf at one or both ends.

Quiver handle. — A 13 cm long handle made of antler (L3:12710), is most likely a quiver handle. In the middle it is narrow and round, flattened towards the ends, and having a vertical hole at each end. At one side, by the hole, is a notch. At one end a 5.5 cm long strap has been attached. This is made of two strips of baleen, bent double and whipped with baleen cord. Another similar strap had, no doubt, been attached at the other end.

Sling handles. — L3:12384, from house 18, is a complete sling handle made of a piece of a wooden bowl. It is 22 cm long, 4.2 cm broad, and has two pairs of deep notches at the front end (cf. I. Pl. 14.18-19). L3:13007 is a broken fore-end of a sling handle made of bone, with three pairs of notches.

Two sling handles for children are of *baleen*. L3:12334 is 17 cm long. L3:12632 has the fore-end broken, but its length had been about 20 cm. Further, a rather weathered specimen, L3:13136, must also have been about 20 cm long.

Bolas. — Three bola balls, rather roughly made, resembling those in I. Pl. 10.15-16, were found. One is of walrus ivory, two are of bone.

Leister harpoon (?) of baleen. — L3:12335, shown on Pl. 1.22, is, possibly, the head of a leister harpoon. — None of the common leister prongs of bone were found.

Gull hooks. — Eleven more or less complete wooden gull hooks, all with an oblique groove for the barb, like that in I. Pl. 14.1. L3:12711 has a barb made of a bird's bone, lashed on with baleen cord and attached to a 1.1 m long baleen line ending in a loop. On L3:12137 and 12943 the barb is of walrus ivory. To the former belongs a large bundle of baleen line; the latter is wrapped up in a lump of blubber from which only the end of the barb and a piece of the baleen line protrude.

Means of commucation.

Toboggan (?). — L3:12485, is a heavy piece of baleen 108 cm long and 12—14 cm broad, with undercut channels in three places, as shown in fig. 40. a. To the channel farthest to the left a piece of strong baleen line (not shown on the figure) was attached, forming a loop 7 cm long. In the channel to the right there are also remains of a baleen line. L3:12484, fig. 40.b, is a similar piece. Apparently it had been longer, but is broken at one of the channels. In addition to the undercut channels, two holes have been drilled through from side to side at the undamaged end.

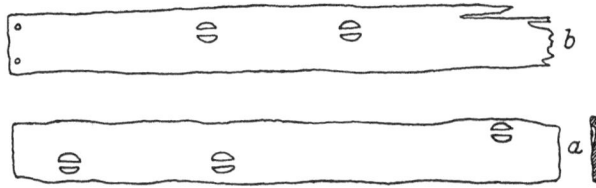

Fig. 40. Parts of toboggan (?) of baleen, from Nûgdlît house 20.

It looks as if several such pieces had been connected. Of course they may have been used for a door or the like, but in that case it would seem unnecessary to have made such elaborate holes or channels. More probably they are pieces of a toboggan, requiring a plain underside; although, to be sure, they lack the characteristic pointed form, as seen e. g. in Boas: "The Eskimo of Baffin Land and Hudson Bay" (1901), fig. 95. Both pieces were found in the passage of house 20.

Sledge runners. — L3:13015 is presumably a fragment, 11.5 cm long, of a *low sledge runner* made of bone. It has a transverse hole near the much worn under side, and on each side a hole can be seen, which has not been bored right through. L3:13085 is a 7 cm long fragment of a small sledge runner of walrus ivory. It is 4 cm broad and 2 cm high, with a transverse hole. The under side is obviously worn, with longitudinal scratches. L3:12755 is a similar fragment, 3.5 cm broad, with two transverse holes for lashings. This appears from the fact that the edges are rounded, and that on the dirty surface marks made by lashing lines can be seen. It is 1.8 cm high and 6 cm long, and broken at one of the holes. A flat strip has been cut away from the under side.

L3:12110, 12511, 12764 and 13116 are presumably fragments of *high sledge runners* made of bone, of a type resembling that shown in I. fig. 103.4. All are broken at a large, cut out hole. L3:12110, seen in fig. 41, is a fore-end. Next to the upper edge are two lashing holes with grooves leading upwards. The runner is made a little thinner in this place. Below there are one oblong and two circular, transverse holes, with grooves for lashings leading downwards. This suggests that the runner was provided with a separate, lashed on shoe. This is corroborated by the fact that the straight underside of the runner is roughly fashioned by hewing, with no marks of wear, whereas the foremost, slanting part is distinctly rounded. — L3:12511 also has one end slanting, it also, no doubt, being a fore-end. L3:13116 has the end fashioned at right angles and thus, presumably, is a rear end. L3:12764 is a fragment 11 cm long, split off from the under part of a runner. It has a large,

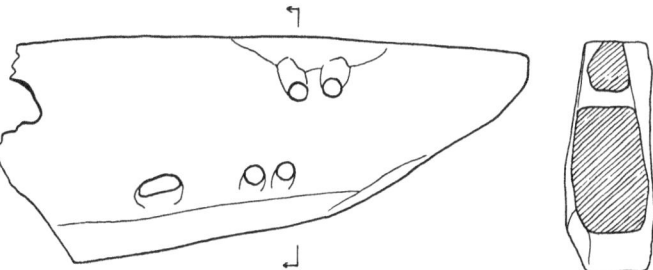

Fig. 41. Fore- end of sledge runner, from Nûgdlît house 6.

cut out hole, a transverse hole, and a slanting hole, apparently part of a curved, transverse channel.

Sledge shoes. — Six fragments of sledge shoes found are of bone, of breadth up to 7 cm. One piece 2.8 cm broad is made of walrus ivory. A piece (L3:13164) made by splitting a narwhal tooth also seems to have been used as a sledge shoe. Five of the specimens mentioned have longitudinally arranged pairs of holes for lashing, but a few oblique plug holes prove that this method of securing the shoes had been used at the same time.

Of baleen sledge shoes 12 pieces were found, up to one meter in length, and up to 9 cm in breadth. They had been fastened both with plugs and lashings through pairs of holes placed longitudinally, or transversally. — No wooden pegs for sledge shoes were found.

Sledge cross-slats. — Eight specimens of whale bone, most of them roughly fashioned and having one or two pairs of opposite notches at the ends (cf. I. Pl. 15.2, 10). Only two of the specimens are complete, these being 51 cm long. A single, broken end (L3:13050), is of a more carefully made cross-slat. It tapers towards the end, which, at its extremity has a knob on each side, as a support for the lashing. On the upper side a longitudinally cut groove runs to the end as a passage for the lashing line when finally it is wound around the upper part of the lashing already made. This is still commonly done by the Polar Eskimos.

In this way they manage to get the lashings extremely tight. — A cut off end of a piece of wood, L3:12650, 3.7 cm broad and 2.5 cm thick, with two wide, transversal grooves at the end and a plain rest on the under side is presumably also a cross slat.

A heavy, curved piece of antler, L3:12926, seen in fig. 42, may have been the foremost, curved cross-slat of a sledge, to which the traces were fastened. It is 35.5 cm long. It looks as if one end had been broken, but then again rounded and provided with a faint groove for a lashing. The other end is flattened and has a ledge at its extremity. The piece has 13 transversal holes. The two penultimate holes at the

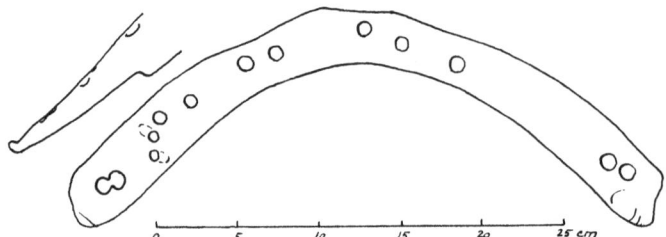

Fig. 42. Sledge cross-slat (?), from house 29, Nûgdlît.

undamaged end slant outwards. In the convex side a narrow groove, 4 cm deep has been cut, most likely, however, without any relevance to the primary use of the object.

Toggle for draught line. — A 4.1 cm long and 1.4 cm broad, roughly fashioned piece of wood, L3:12834, a little narrower in the middle, is most likely a toggle for the draught line.

Trace buckles. — Of eight specimens, all rather roughly made, seven are of walrus ivory, one of narwhal tusk. All are of the common type with two parallel holes, like that shown in I. Pl. 16.26. — L3:12911 is of bone, more carefully made, resembling that in I. Pl. 16.27. — Two specimens, L3:12415 and 12833, both of walrus ivory, have the holes at right angles, as in I. Pl. 16.25.

Umiaq. — Two pieces of heavy skin, of irregular shape, L3:12899. a-b, found in house 28, no doubt are cut off pieces of an *umiaq* cover. Both have long, double, watertight seams. On one piece slits about one centimeter long have been cut along the long edges at intervals of 2—2.5 cm, and in one place remains of a kind of baleen thread seam can be seen, the thread passing twice through the slit, then over the edge, and again twice through the next slit. The piece is roughly oval in shape, and also has a small slit cut at one of the ends. For what purpose the skin piece thus fashioned had been used, is unknown.

A curious, cleft piece of bone, L3:12328, from house 16, seen in fig. 43, is presumably a *harpoon rest*, placed at the bow of an umiaq

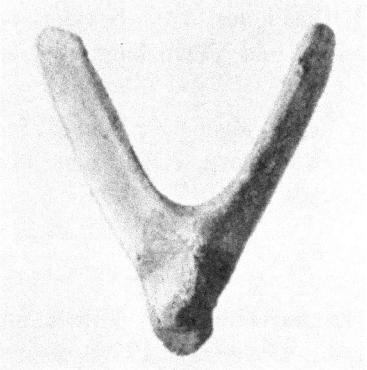

Fig. 43. Harpoon rest for umiaq (?), from Nûgdlît house 16.

for whale hunting. It is 12 cm high, the two branches being 4.5 cm broad. It is made of a naturally cleft bone, with the lower part made into an oblong, tapering tenon.

A pointed, curved piece of bone, L3:12108, from house 6, seen in fig. 44, is most likely a barb for a *boat-hook*. The scarf and holes at the

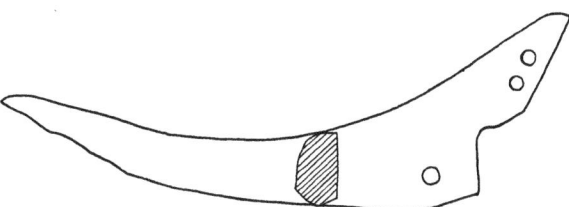

Fig. 44. Boat-hook, from house 6, Nûgdlît.

butt indicate that the object had been attached to a rod with the concave side outwards.

Kayak deck beams (?). — 11 specimens, made of curved pieces of bone, are possibly kayak deck beams. This I found the most plausible interpretation when treating similar objects found at Thule and on the Ruinø (cf. I. p. 231 f.), but the final proof can not be given as yet[1]). The convex sides of the bone pieces have been made plain, and at the undamaged ends a groove for a lashing can be seen. Most of them have the characteristic obliquely placed pairs of holes, as shown in I. fig.

---

[1]) A possibility which also might be taken into consideration is that they may have been cross-slats for low sledges of the type still in use among the western Eskimos.

103.12-13. Only two specimens are without holes. One of these, L3:12207, has only one end broken, and the length can thus be seen to have been about 37 cm. L3:13221 had been of about the same length. To judge from the placing of the holes, two heavier pieces, L3:13173 and 12206, had been about 40 and 44 cm long, corresponding to the specimens described in I. p. 231.

End mounting for kayak paddle. — L3:13174, found in ruin 56, is an end mounting of walrus ivory, 7 × 2.7 cm. It belonged to a kayak paddle with a broad blade end.

Tools.

Snow knife. — The parts of snow knives found prove that they had been of the compound type. L3:12418, seen on Pl. 2.5, is a handle of wood with a bed for a heavy blade, which, most likely, had been of bone (cf. Th. Mathiassen 1927. I. Pl. 15.9). L3:12653 is a cut off piece of a handle of antler, with a slit for the blade and a large lashing hole, of a type resembling that in I. Pl. 18.11. L3:12835 is a curved blade of walrus ivory, 27.5 cm long. As the rear end is broken, it cannot be seen how it had been attached to the handle. Further, two small fragments of similar snow knife blades of walrus ivory were found.

A broken end of a round bone stick with an oblong, egg-shaped extension, (L3:12281), is probably the butt of a *snow probe* (cf. I. Pl. 17.16).

L3:12927 seems to be the rear end of a *snow shovel blade* (cf. I. Pl. 17.8). It is one centimeter thick, and the breadth decreases to 5 cm at the rear end. It has a faintly hollowed rest for the shaft, and two pairs of lashing holes.

Knives. — *Knives with end-blades.* — All specimens belonging to this main type have a slot for a blade in the end. A total of 31 complete or fragmentary specimens were found, of which 20 are of bone, 7 of antler, 3 of musk-ox horn, and 1 of walrus ivory. 29 are of the type shown in I. Pl. 19.7-16; lengths 9—19 cm. Most have the fore-end a little widened. Pl. 1.27 is a fine handle of musk-ox horn. At the fore-end it has a lashing of plaited sinews. Twelve of the handles have a transverse hole in the butt for a strap. On two specimens the hole is bored from one side to the butt, and on one, L3:12308, which has a wedge-shaped butt, the hole leads from one side to the other, i. e. in the plane of the blade. One specimen, L3:12417, has a slot for a blade at both ends. — L3:12444 is a blade end of a knife handle of bone with a scarf, apparently for lashing on to a longer handle. L3:12432 is most likely another such handle, of wood, 13 cm long, with a rounded butt and a hole for a strap. The blade end has a scarf and a wide groove for a lashing, and roughly in the middle are two holes for plugs. L3:12445 is also a butt with a scarf. — Eight of the specimens, lengths 9—10 cm, are, no doubt, handles of *whittling knives*.

Of the type with *the handle made of two halves*, four specimens were found, two of them of walrus ivory, one of antler, and one of bone, resembling that in I. Pl. 20.2. In L3:12642 the remains of an iron blade can be seen.

L3:12979 is a split off piece from the fore-end of the handle of a *flensing knife*. It is made of bone, with an open end slit for the blade, and a plug hole (cf. I. Pl. 20.2).

Knife with side blade. — Only one specimen of a primitive form was found, consisting of a piece of willow twig 9 cm long, with a 3 cm long slit placed two centimeters from one end. Traces of vivianite prove that it had an iron blade.

Knife blades of iron. — Six flat pieces of iron can, with some certainty, be identified as knife blades. In those cases where an analysis has been possible they have proved to be of meteoric iron. L3:12152 is 7×2.3 cm, with a rounded fore-end, and with the rear end tapering a little. L3:12605 is 5×3 cm, with a hole placed a little to one side. An elongated oval blade, L3:12880, 6×2.3 cm, is most likely from an ulo.

Bone knife. — L3:12400 may be a knife used for squeezing out water from hairy skins. It is of antler, slightly S-curved and rather roughly made; 23 cm long and 1.8 cm broad. The blade part has an edge on both sides. The fore-end is flattened and rounded. — L3:12221 is a broken end of a knife-like tool of walrus ivory, 2.25 cm broad, with an edge on both sides.

Baleen knife. — Three one-edged knives are of baleen, length 19—20 cm, breadth 2.2—4 cm. Of these L3:13064 is similar to that shown in I. Pl. 49.15. L3:12819 is almost identical, except that the handle narrows-in more. L3:12407 is of a type resembling that in I. Pl. 49.12, but the transition from blade to handle is marked only by two notches opposite one another.

A *spatula-shaped* tool of baleen, shown on Pl. 2.7, has the broad part provided with sharp edges. Apparently it is a knife.

Hand drill. — L3:12982, Pl. 2.3, is a drill handle of antler. In the end which on the figure is on the left, there is a hole, 0.2 cm wide, most likely for an iron bit.

A wooden handle-like object, L3:12644, was found in house 24.B. It is 6.8 cm long, of oval cross-section about 1.8×1.4 cm, and with the butt rounded. In the fore-end it has a hole, which is 0.7 cm wide and almost as deep as the full length of the handle. Around the fore-end there is a groove for a lashing. For what purpose this object had been used is not quite clear, but it may have been as a kind of hand drill.

Bow drill. — L3:12387 is a heavy *drill shank* of bone, 14 cm long, with a hole 3 cm deep and about 0.5 cm wide, in the fore-end. A deep groove, 5 cm long, widening towards the end, runs to the rear end, the shank apparently having been lengthened with an extra piece. — L3:12204 is a fragment of a *drill foreshaft* of antler, 8 cm long, with a tetrahedral rear end, for insertion into a wooden shank, (cf. I. Pl. 24.22-23, which only differ in having a scarf).

Only one *drill mouthpiece* was found: L3:12645. It is a large caribou astragalus, quite worn through, (cf. I. Pl. 24.25).

Whetstones. — 11 specimens, of which three are of a reddish, fine-grained sandstone, as in I. Pl. 29.29. L3:12501 is 29 cm long, with a cross section about 3×3 cm. L3:12612 is about $29 \times 9 \times 3$ cm, with grinding surfaces on the two long, narrow sides only.

Hammer stones. — 19 specimens of the type shown in I. Pl. 29.27, length 8—16 cms.

Flint flakers. — 24 complete specimens, in addition to two broken fore-ends. Of these 15 are from *ribs* (cf. I. Pl. 27.12), one, L3:12448, of *walrus penis-bone*. Two specimens are of *bone* with a wedge-shaped fore-end. L3:12348 is of *antler*. Seven are of *walrus ivory*, L3:12713 and 12912 being made from a whole tooth, lengths 31 and 33 cm. On L3:12713 the fore-end is sharply wedge-shaped, 1.4 cm broad at the point, and curving a little upwards, the concave upper side thus forming a convenient rest for the thumb. L3:12352 is made from a piece of walrus ivory, about 12 cm long and almost square in cross-section, 1.2×1.2 cm. The fore end is flattened and has a concavity, made by flaking off a broad splinter. — A large *bear's tooth*, 9.3 cm long, (L3:12932), from the fore-end of which some flakes have been split off, bears the marks of wear characteristic of flint flakers.

Stone maul heads. — Five specimens, of which four have a roughly fashioned, vertical edge. L3:12451 is of a thick wedge-shape, due to the natural cleavage of the stone. Its size is $18.5 \times 6 \times 6.3$ cm. L3:13090 is about $11 \times 6.5 \times 2.5$ cm. L3:12391 and 12392 are flat, more like axe blades, about 19 cm long. The breadths of the rear ends are 11 and 12 cm, of the fore-ends about 9 cm. The thickness is about 3 and 2.5 cm, decreasing towards the front. On L3:12391 the middle part of one long side is also fashioned into a rough edge.

L3:13212, found in ruin 59, shown in fig. 45, is of a *pestle-like* type. The fore-end is rounded, the rear part narrower than the front, with the end rounded. — There is no indication that the maul heads had been provided with handles, as was the case with e. g. the maul in I. Pl. 28.5.

A cut off piece of bone of an angular shape, 24 cm long, (L3:12815), had probably been used as a *blubber pounder*.

Adzes. — Seven *adze heads* all of bone, with a wide socket for a stone blade. Four of the specimens have *no lashing holes*, (cf. I. Pl. 28.9). L3:13154 and 13178, which are of this type, are crudely made. L3:12201 has the characteristic pentagonal cross-section, like those in I. Pl. 28.15-16. — L3:12499 has four *vertical lashing holes* which on the upper side are connected in twos by transversal grooves. The butt is

Fig. 45. Stone pestle, from ruin 59, Nûgdlît.

rounded. — Two specimens have *horizontal lashing holes* like that in I. Pl. 28.13. L3:13089 had three holes, but is cut off at the end one. L3:12643 has two holes and between them a groove for a lashing.

Three *adze handles*, of which two are of bone and one of antler, have a wide lashing hole like that in I. Pl. 28.20. L3:12841, of antler, has the butt broken, but the other two specimens have a unilateral knob on the concave side. — One adze head of antler, (L3:12500), has three holes, like that in I. Pl. 28.19, and on another, fragmentary specimen, the three holes have been merged into onle large hole.

Hand picks. — Two complete specimens and two fragments of slender ribs, resembling that in I. Pl. 30.7. L3:12091 is 23 cm long, made of a heavier rib. L3:12723 is of whale bone with the fore-end flattened. L3:12205 is made from a small walrus penis bone.

Pick-axe heads. — L3:12397 is a 12.5 cm long, broken fore-end of a *hatchet* of walrus ivory (cf. I. Pl. 30.6). It has two transverse holes, placed 9.5 and 11.5 cm from the point. On the outer side several irregular, longitudinal scratches can be seen. The under side has been flattened by crude cross hewing. L3:12588 is a broken fore-end, of a similar hatchet 15.5 cm long, but made of bone. It seems to have been broken at an indentation for a lashing.

L3:12154 is a pick-axe head, hewed from a piece of whale rib. It has a crudely rounded shape with a strong point. Its max. length is 37.5 cm with a cross-section of about 3.3 × 2.7 cm. Seven centimeters from the blunt rear end there is a whipping of baleen cord. L3:13158 is a piece of a pick-axe head, or pointed mattock head 48 cm long, and made of whale bone with a flatter cross-section; the rear end is broken.

Mattocks. — Five fragments of heavy *mattock heads* were found, all of whale bone. Four are fore-ends, and one a rear end with a bed for the handle and three pairs of deep lashing notches. L3:12208 has the rear end broken, but a new bed has been made, its edges being roughened by hewing. — Two fore-ends of *mattock handles* have an oblong lashing hole as in I. Pl. 30.11.

Six *chopping blocks* of whale vertebrae and one from a piece of a large whale bone.

Eleven *wedges* of bone 5—24 cm long.

Marline spikes. — Three marline spikes found are of the pointed type. Two of these are of bone. L3:12470 is of antler and has a hole in the broad butt. — L3:12430, of walrus ivory, has the fore-end flattened and rounded. The lengths of the specimens vary from 9 to 12 cm.

L3:12523 is a *pointed ulna*, length 14.5 cm. — L3:13175 is made from a *fibula*. It is 17 cm long and has one end flattened and the point rounded, like that in I. Pl. 29.10. In the thick rear part a deep groove has been cut all the way round.

Bone nails. — Five specimens, 1.8—3.7 cm long. Four of them are of walrus ivory, one of bone. The longest specimen is four-sided with a slight, head-like extension.

Ulos. — Seven ulo handles were found, five of them of bone, two of wood. L3:12502 is a small, roughly fashioned wooden handle, 6.2 cm long and 2 cm high, with a 4 cm long iron blade. L3:12726, also of wood, is shown on Pl. 2.1. It is crescent-shaped with a concave blade edge, 11 cm long. It has a 5 cm long groove for a stone blade, and two lashing holes. — L3:13141 is a small, regularly shaped handle of bone, 6 × 3.2 cm, resembling that shown in I. Pl. 22.14, but having a straighter back. The under side is 4.3 cm long with a narrow blade groove only 2 cm long. — L3:12261 is almost trapezoidal with a thick, convex back, almost like that in I. Pl. 22.20. — L3:12914, shown on Pl. 2.2, has a long, cut out hole. The blade groove is wide and about the full length of the lower edge. — Two fragments of rather thin ulo handles, lengths 8.7—11.5 cm, also have oblong openings which are, however, more irregular. On one of the specimens, (L3:13097), the lower edge is concave.

Flint scraper with convex edge. — Only one specimen was found, L3:12727, 3.6 × 3.6 cm. It is rather crudely made with the butt narrowed in a little; (cf. I. Pl. 2.29).

Ground scraper of flint. — Pl. 1.20 is a peculiar, small implement of flint, about 3 × 1.4 × 0.4 cm. The rounded end and one long edge have been fashioned by flaking, the two other edges and the two plain sides being ground, thus forming a sharp right-angled edge along one side and two long facets at the end. The small, concave indentation has no scraping edge, indicating that this end was inserted into a handle. The implement thus seems to have been used as a side scraper for wood and bone. In fact, its efficiency has been demonstrated by experiment.

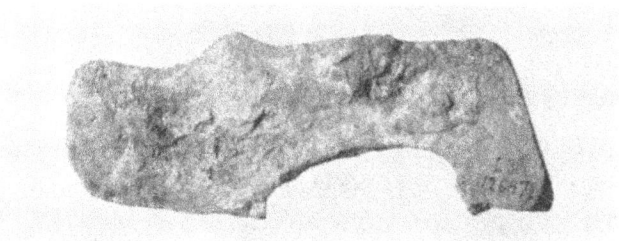

Fig. 46. Stone scraper, from house 24.B, Nûgdlît.

Blunt stone scrapers. — L3:12647, fig. 46, is made of a flat stone, shaped so as to form a convenient handle. Its length is 18 cm. — Two natural, flat stones have also been used as blunt scrapers. One, L3:12041, is an elongated oval, about 5.6 × 2.8 × 1.3 cm, rounded, and having several fine, longitudinal scratches on one side. L3:12042 is more irregularly four-sided, about 6 × 2.2 × 1 cm, with a rather sharp scraping edge on one side.

Bone scrapers. — 12 specimens of bone, one of antler, and two of walrus ivory which had apparently been used as scrapers for skin softening. Most of them are atypical, rather crudely fashioned; length 4—19.5 cm. Their fore-ends are narrow and rounded, almost as in I. Pl. 26.17. L3:12719 is the most regular specimen. It is a flat wedge-shape, made from a curved piece of antler, length 15.5 cm, breadth 3—3.6 cm. Six of the specimens are quite short, up to 7.5 cm long, with all edges rounded by wear. L3:12475 is made of a slender walrus molar, 4.7 cm long.

Two-handed scrapers. — Three specimens of walrus penis bone, as in I. Pl. 27.1. Of these L3:12848 is 42 cm long, with two sets of scraping edges on opposite sides. The thick part of the bone has been made thinner by hewing off from one side, and the spongy part has been removed, thus forming a deep groove leading from the scraping part towards the end. The two other specimens are broken ends. On L3:12153 the fractured end has been rounded, and it seems to have been used as a flint flaker.

Cup-shaped scrapers. — Two specimens, both of walrus ivory. L3:12916 has a curved canal for a string on the outer side of the bottom, as shown in I. Pl. 24.2.

L3:12811 is a fragment of a *fat scraper* with a long, *straight*, sharp edge, made from a shoulder blade (or pelvis?). The flat part with the edge is only 0.1 cm thick.

A scraper, L3:12210, made from a piece of the hollow root end of a walrus tusk, is most likely a *urine scraper*. Its size is 6 × 2.5 × 1.3 cm.

Sewing needle. — L3:12812 is a broken butt of a sewing needle of walrus ivory. It has a flat triangular cross-section, 0.45 × 0.15 cm, and has a circular hole at the end.

Bodkin. — A 6.2 cm long, thin, pointed bodkin, L3:12728, made of a bird's bone. The butt is broken.

Thimbles. — Three specimens of skin of the common type with a slit for the index, as shown in I. Pl. 36.20. One of the specimens, L3:12169, has been cut out with an extra, regularly heptagonal appendage, which folded up makes the thimble double so as to resist the pressure of the needle better.

Household utensils.

Pyrites had been commonly used for striking fire, a total of 65 pieces being found. The surroundings of Nûgdlît are still known as a source of pyrite.

Lamps. — Only four fragments of soap-stone lamps were found. Three of these are from rather large and heavy lamps. To which type

Fig. 47. Profile of lamp fragment, from Nûgdlît house 26.

they belong could not be ascertained with safety, but none of the specimens show any traces of a partition ledge or knobs. The largest specimen, L3:12747, has a step five centimeters from the front edge, as seen in fig. 47. L3:12063 is a corner of a small lamp, resembling that shown in I. Pl. 32.4, but with the front edge almost straight. Along the front edge, at a distance of about one centimeter, a faint line has been scratched.

Thirty of the *lamp trimmers* found are wooden sticks; eight are pieces of willow branches.

Cooking pots. 71 — fragments of soap-stone cooking pots were found, a few of which could be put together into larger pieces. Only L3:12730

Fig. 48. Profile of pottery lamp fragment, from Nûgdlît house 31.

is almost complete. It is a small, low, crudely made pot, 10.5 cm long, 8.1 cm wide, and 3.8 cm high, of a rounded rectangular shape like that in I. Pl. 43.15. L3:12064 is a fragment of a small, unfinished, oval pot, 7.3 cm wide and 5.2 cm high; its length had been about 15 cm. — The other fragments are from larger pots, of shapes similar to those mentioned, i. e. a type with almost straight, or only slightly curved sides, with only the ends more rounded; and a second rounder type. The first mentioned type seems to have been the predominant one. — On most specimens, where part of the rim is preserved, the rim is simply rounded. On one fragment belonging to L3:12547 there is an incised line on the inner side, about one centimeter from the upper edge. One specimen, L3:12156, has a cut out, oblong suspension hole, and three fragments have projections on the inner side with one or two holes leading up obliquely through the upper edge. Of the latter, L3:12503 is a corner of a fairly big, but rather low pot. Judging from the curvature it could hardly have been more than 6 or 6.5 cm high.

Pottery. — L3:13054.b is an 8 × 8 × 2.4—3 cm fragment of a rounded pot, with a thick layer of soot on the outside and a crust of food on the inside. — L3:13054.a is about 8 × 5.5 × 1.9 cm with part of the rounded rim preserved. Its shape suggests that it is from a lamp. Both specimens are made of a clay-like substance in which among other things small stones are imbedded. The specimens show a stratified structure with layers parallel to the surface. On the lamp fragment the layers can be seen to follow the curve of the rim, as shown in fig. 48. This proves that at least the outer part of the rim had been built up of flat strips of clay which have successively been bent down around the edge and merged together.

Meat tray. — Only four small fragments of meat trays were found. These are hollowed out of wood and have thin sides.

Oval bowls. — Three complete bowl sides of baleen. The ends of the baleen strips, from which they are made, are joined by baleen stitching. The sizes range from about 35 × 25 to 18 × 9 cm, the heights of all the specimens being almost the same: about 9 cm. On two fragments it can be seen how the overlapping ends have been sewn together by two rows of stitches. The seam next to the inner, vertical edge of the baleen strip is made with long stitches running parallel to the edge, whereas the outer edge is sewn "over and over", because the jointing on the convex side would otherwise be apt to gape.

Three *oval bowl bottoms* are of bone, and two of baleen. L3:13056 is a complete bottom of bone, almost circular, 37.5 × 35 cm. The two bottoms of baleen are 20 × 12 and 17.5 × 10 cm. The latter, L3:12138, had been used as a cutting board.

A *wooden ladle*, L3:12552, from house 23, is 23 cm long and 8.5 cm broad in front, resembling that in I. Pl. 34.5. L3:12918 is a *ladle of musk-ox horn*, as in I. Pl. 34.8, but the handle is missing. It was found in house 29, filled with refuse, blubber, small bones and flattened remains of egg shells, etc.

Fish spoon (?) of baleen. — The implement shown on Pl. 2.4 suggests a fish spoon most of all. It has a frame, made of a baleen strip 0.7 cm broad, bent over and lashed, thus forming a figure 8, the straight ends forming a handle. The outer sides of the figure 8 are connected on each side by a baleen cord, and the whole frame has been filled out with a netting of thin baleen threads loosely slung together. The total length is now 22.5 cm, the end of the handle being damaged. The blade part is about 4.5 × 9 cm.

Meat stick. — Four bone sticks, three of which are from split ribs with rounded points, length 25.5—14 cm, have most likely been used as meat sticks. — A crudely made, pointed stick of whale bone, (L3:12401), 32.5 cm long, is probably a *blubber fork*. The same applies to four pointed wooden sticks and two of baleen.

Carrying stick. — A cut off, somewhat tapering end of a flat baleen rod, 2 cm broad, (L3:12799), has two deep notches opposite one another and may be a fragment of a carrying stick like that in I. Pl. 48.16.

Baleen handles. — Two fragments are of handles made of narrow baleen strips, bent double and whipped with similar strips.

Pot hook. — A small hook of walrus ivory with a suspension hole, shown on Pl. 1.13, is most likely a pot hook. The end is broken.

Edge mounting. — L3:12399 is a 15 cm long, broken end of a 3—2.3 cm broad edge mounting of bone. The outer side is convex, the inner side concave with a longitudinal groove at the broken end. At a distance of 6 cm from the end there is a plug hole, and next to the end the outer side is roughened and provided with a transverse projection as a support for a lashing. Its use is unknown.

Clothing, toilet articles, etc.

Gutskin jackets. — In house 28 several large pieces of gutskin jackets were found. Only after careful treatment in the laboratory of the National Museum were the fragile skins made sufficiently pliable for careful handling. The garments were much torn, but they proved to be the greater part of three jackets, the cut of which could be fairly well ascertained. — L3:12893 is the best preserved. On fig. 49.A it is seen from the front, and folded except for the hood part. Fig. 50 shows the back side in the same manner. On fig. 49.B the hood and shoulder part are seen from the side and from above respectively, drawn in one plane. Similarly fig. 49.C shows the under side of the sleeve and the adjoining part of the body. The jacket was found with the inside turned out. It is made of long strips of gutskin running lengthwise, and lengthened at the bottom with a wide strip made of 10—15 cm long pieces sewn together. The lower edge is trimmed with a strip of depilated sealskin one centimeter broad. In the front and back the jacket ends in broad, rounded flaps, the back flap being about 25 cm longer than the front flap. The whole length of the jacket, from the top to the lower edge, is about 105 cm in the front, and 130 cm at the back.

The central piece of the jacket is a strip about 12 cm broad, reaching from one shoulder, across the crown of the hood, and down to the other shoulder. Upon this yoke the rest of the jacket had been suspended, as it were. The yoke consists of two pieces of equal lengths, sewn together at the crown. The two median strips in front divide into two branches a little beneath the chin, where a triangular throat piece had been inserted, and proceed up around the opening for the face, being here 5 cm broad and being sewn to the yoke. The free edge, together with the upper edge of the throat piece, form the hood opennig, which, all the way round, has a border consisting of a strip of depilated sealskin, about 0.7 cm broad. One long strip and a broad gore are also attached to the yoke on each side of the front median strips, the gore being inserted in order to give more width at the breast. Further down two narrower gores are inserted. On each side of this front part of the jacket a long strip has been added, running over the shoulder, where it is sewn to the end of the yoke, and down the back. The greater part of the sleeves are directly sewn on to the outer edges of these strips. The back is made in a corresponding manner, except that the two median strips stop at the neck, where the nape of the hood begins. The nape

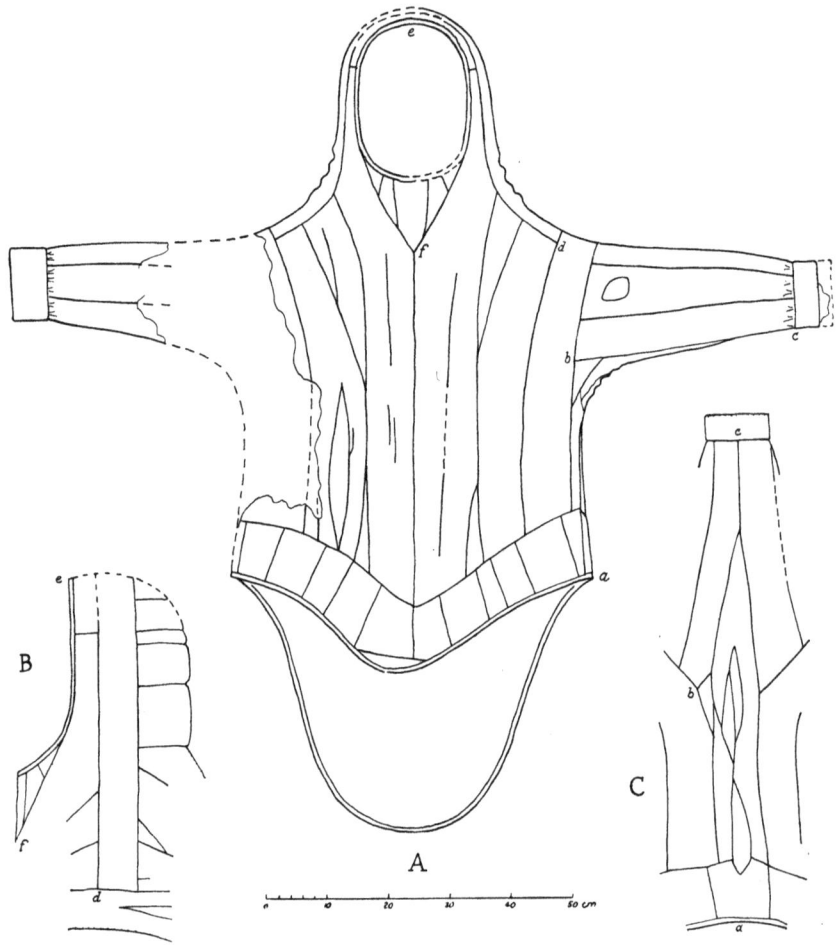

Fig. 49. Gutskin jacket, L3:12893, from Nûgdlît. (A) front view; (B) side of hood, and shoulder part; (C) under side of sleeve.

is composed of horizontal strips, sewn to the yoke and adjusted to fit the rounding of the nape, as seen in fig. 49. B.

The length of the sleeves, as measured from the armpits, had been about 40 cm. The sleeves are made of long strips, which have been somewhat gathered at the wristband. The latter is made of a strip of gutskin 6 cm broad. The innermost part of the under side of the sleeve consists of a broad gore piece which extends from the side of the body out into the sleeve, as shown on fig. 49. C. The gore is made by partly splitting a broad strip and filling the gap thus made with several smaller gores.

It can be seen on the drawing, that in several places a broad strip of gutskin has median seams which do not extend to the ends of the

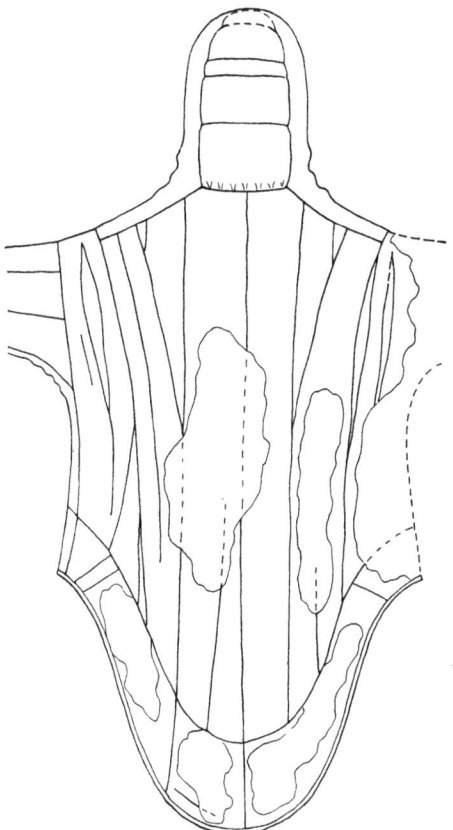

Fig. 50. Gutskin jacket, L3:12893, from Nûgdlît. Back view.

strip. This may be in order to strengthen weaker parts, but in most cases it is probably to prevent bulging, to which sewn gutskin strips have a particular tendency. The seams are all sewn with "overcast" stitches.

L3:12894, fig. 51—52, is more damaged than that described above, but the pattern can be seen to be the same in all essentials. The sleeves, however, seem to have been attached to the body a little differently, but owing to the bad condition of the jacket, the method could not be ascertained. A peculiar feature is that the body is divided into two parts by a horizontal seam, which, however, does not, in principle alter the pattern of the vertical strips. Lower down, the jacket is badly torn, but the front suggests that originally it had flaps corresponding to those of L3:12893. The hood opening has no sealskin border, the edge of the gutskin being only tucked in and sewn with "overcast".

L3:12895, fig. 53—54, is cut off more unevenly at the bottom and the sleeves are lacking, but it seems to have been of a similar pattern

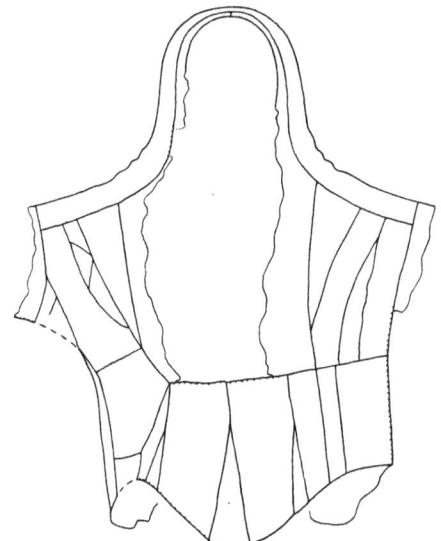

Fig. 51. Gutskin jacket, L3:12894, from Nûgdlît. Front view.

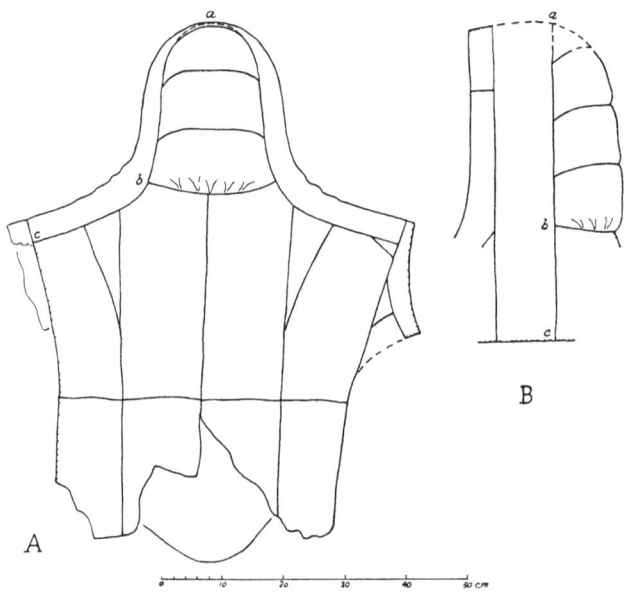

Fig. 52. Gutskin jacket, L3:12894, from Nûgdlît. (A) back view (B) side of hood.

to the other two. No seam can be seen at the bottom edge, but this may be due to the fact that the lowest part has been cut off. In one particular it deviates from the other gutskin jackets found: the nape of the hood is not composed of horizontal strips. Instead of this the two median, vertical strips of the back continue right up to the crown.

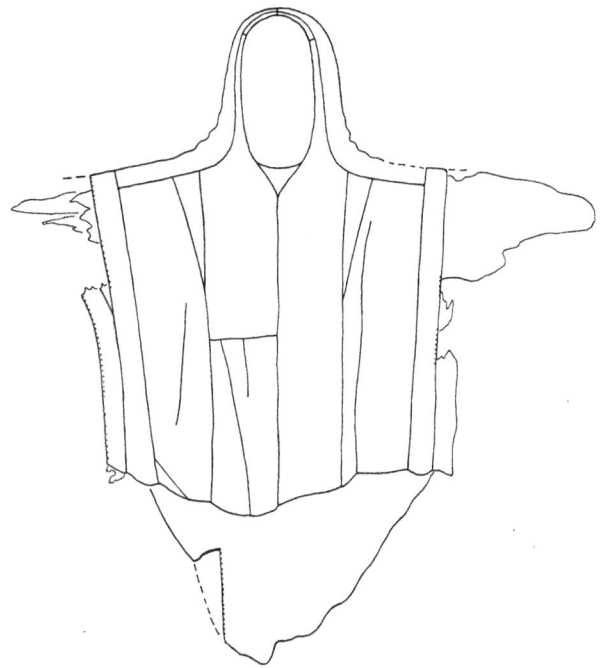

Fig. 53. Gutskin jacket, L3:12895, from Nûgdlît. Front view.

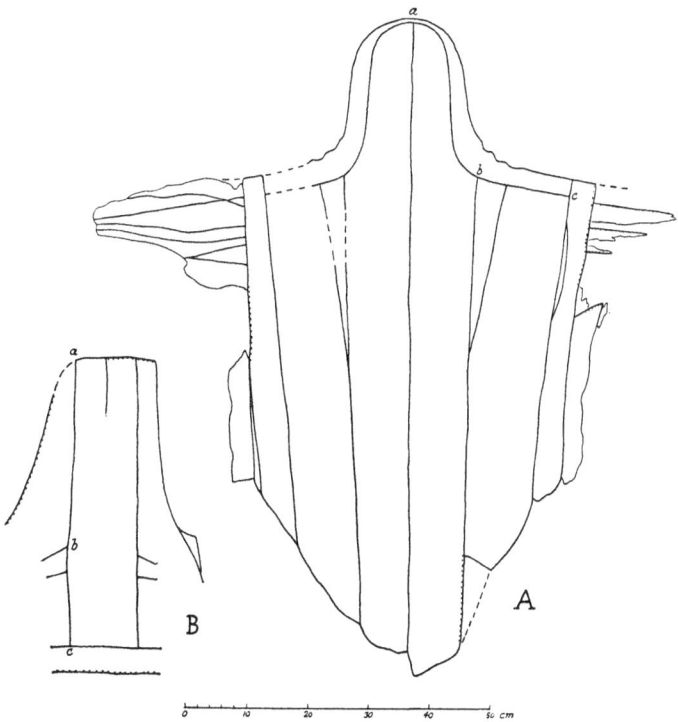

Fig. 54. Gutskin jacket, L3:12895, from Nûgdlît. (A) back view; (B) side of the hood.

The head opening is similar to that of L3:12894, i. e. lacking the sealskin border.

In house 22 a small fragment (L3:12538) was found, which seems to be the rounded flap of a gutskin jacket with a narrow border of hairy sealskin.

Birdskin jacket. — L3:12896.a is a fragment of a birdskin jacket, about 30 × 40 cm, with part of the lower edge preserved. As far as can be seen it had a rounded flap. An irregularly cut strip of dogskin, about 1.5 cm broad, is sewn on to the lower edge. The skins used look like gullskins or the like.

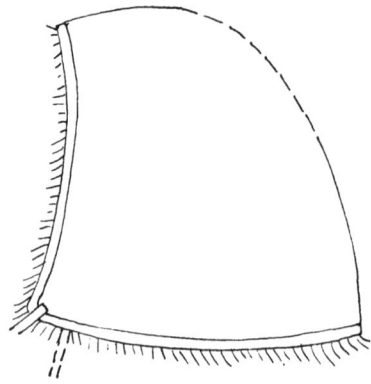

Fig. 55. Loose hood of birdskin, from Nûgdlît house 28.

Loose hood of birdskin. — L3:12896.b is a hood of birdskin with the downy side inwards. It is seen in fig. 55, with the opening to the left. It is open at the chin. At each corner remnants of a sewn-on skin strip can be seen, apparently used to tie the hood together under the chin. At one side the chin band is placed just at the corner, at the other side about 6 cm from it along the neck edge, so as to make the lower parts of the hood overlap a little. All along the edge is a border consisting of a strip of dogskin one centimeter broad. The hood was found rolled up in a bundle, tied with a narrow skin strip 52 cm long.

Birdskin trousers (?). — L3:12896.c, shown in fig. 56, seems to be part of a child's trousers or the like, made of birdskin with the feathery side inwards. The lower, untorn part no doubt forms the trouser leg. The back side of the trouser leg is suggested by the obvious wear on the outside and the torn-off feathers on the inside. Thus, in fig. 56.a the piece is seen from one side, the knee to the right. On fig. 56.b it lies unfolded, showing what is preserved of the upper part. At the back of the knee the feathers are completely worn off, and low down they have become matted, whereas in front the plumage is full. A depression in the feathers seems to indicate the position of the knee. On the back side, well up the thigh, the trousers have apparently burst. — This interpretation rests on the assumption that the wear is mainly due to sitting—on a sledge or platform. On the lower, closed part, which is about 25 cm long, no longitudinal seam can be seen. Thus this leg piece must have been made of a whole birdskin. At the upper edge two smaller pieces have been added. At the lower edge there is a border of dogskin. As this is of a somewhat irregular shape, it cannot be ascertained with

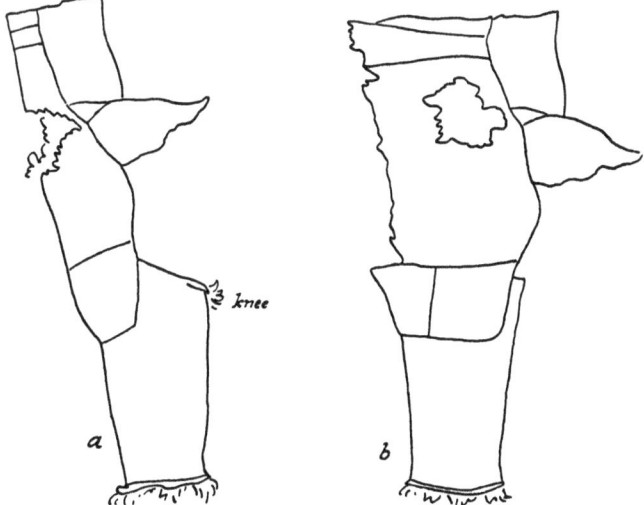

Fig. 56. Fragment of birdskin trousers (?), from Nûgdlît house 28.

safety whether it formed part of a foot, in which case the whole garment must have been a hose. The length of the upper part, above the knee, is about 25 cm. At the upper edge a piece of dogskin had been inserted. As, however, its upper edge is also irregularly cut off, its original size cannot be estimated. The piece found may belong to a pair of trousers, leggings, hose, or a combination suit.

Footwear. — Seven fragments of footwear were found. L3:12897 is the uppermost part of a boot-leg. On fig. 57.B it is seen unfolded. It is of sealskin with the hairs inwards. The lower part is torn off. The watertight, longitudinal seam a—b has presumably been in the front. Above, two narrow, wedge-shaped pieces have been added, sewn together in line with the longitudinal seam. On to these a border of dogskin is sewn. It is only partly preserved, and is composed of several smaller pieces. Only the stretch a—c seems not to have had anything sewn on to it. The total breadth (unfolded) at the top is 50 cm, the length of the preserved piece about 32 cm. Its shape and size suggest a woman's high boot.

L3:12898, (fig. 57.A,) is, no doubt, the cut-off top part of the leg of a woman's high boot or stocking, made of dogskin with the hair inside. Two longitudinal seams prove that the boot-leg has been composed of two pieces of skin, the widths of which, at the top, were 26 and 32 cm. On the widest piece a 34 cm long and 1—1.5 cm broad strip of sealskin with the hairs almost worn off has been sewn on at a distance of 6 cm from one of the longitudinal seams. At the upper end of the strip is a slit 3 cm long, by which the strip was most likely fastened to

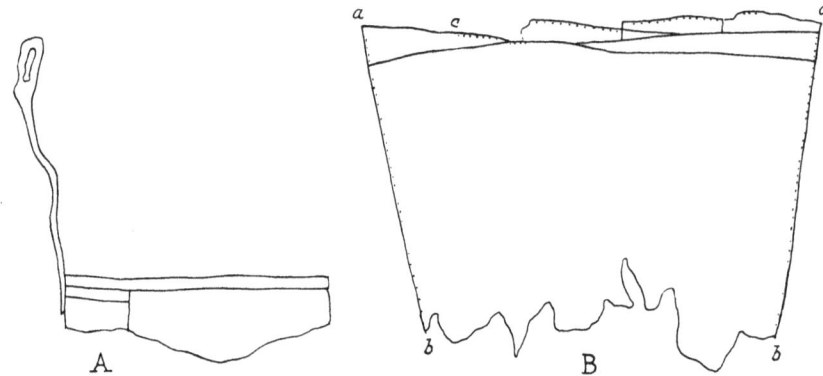

Fig. 57. Fragments of boots, from Nûgdlît house 28.

a button or belt. All along the upper edge of the boot-leg a strip of dogskin 2 cm broad had been sewn on. It had been bent double, and a marginal seam indicates that another strip of skin had been sewn on, probably as a trimming. The height of the boot seems to have been the same all the way round. At the strap, one of the large skin pieces has been eked out with a narrow gore, 12 cm long, apparently in order to make an even upper edge.

L3:12171, fig. 58, is a boot sole of hairy sealskin with the hairy side inwards. Its size is about 26 × 13 cm. On each side it has two projecting laps with eyelets for a lace, the marginal seam of the sole running inside the eyelets. On the under side two large and two smaller patches have been sewn on, the smaller ones being covered totally, or in part by one of the larger patches from which a piece had been cut off. The arrow on the figure indicates the direction of the hairs, this proving that the front of the sole is to the left. — L3:12944 is a similar sole, about 26 × 12 cm, and worn through in two places.

L3:12574 is a cut-off piece of the edge of a heavy skin sole, crudely crimped, and sewn on to what appears to be a dogskin stocking, as the skin forming the upper of the boot shows no edge along the seam, but continues into a sole. — L3:12785.a is a fragment of a boot sole which has been sewn on to a leg of hairy sealskin with the hair inside.

L3:12784.a is a fragment of the foot of a stocking of hairy sealskin, hair inside. Remains of a seam can be seen along the edge of the foot,

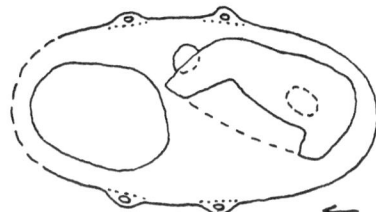

Fig. 58. Boot sole, from house 10, Nûgdlît.

and of another seam above the instep, the upper thus having apparently been made of a separate piece of skin. Inside the toe is a thick layer of *baleen wool*. — Seven other bundles of baleen wool were found.

Mitten. — L3:12786, fig. 59, is a mitten of bearskin with the fur outside. On the inner side of the thumb the fur is quite worn off. The mitten is composed of three pieces, the largest of which forms the back. The edge is bent over, crimped at the finger tips, and sewn on to the

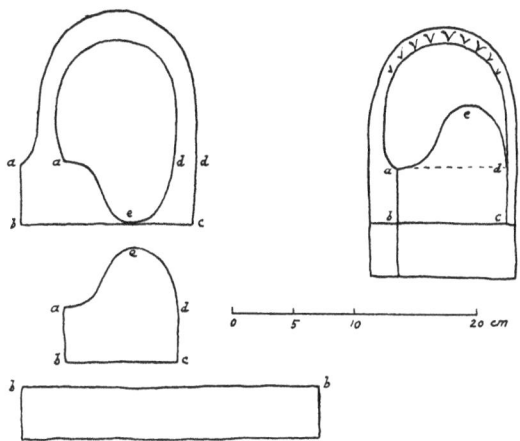

Fig. 59. Mitten of bearskin, from Nûgdlît house 26.

palm piece, an extension of which forms the inner side of the thumb. The third piece forms the back of the thumb. To these is added a wrist piece consisting of a border of bearskin 4 cm broad with the fur inside.

L3:12172 is the thumb and part of the palm of a sealskin mitten with the hair outside, and of the same pattern as above. L3:12784.b is a fragment of a child's mitten with the thumb torn off, also of the same pattern. The back is made of depilated sealskin, the palm of sealskin with the hair inside. The wrist has a border made of a strip of hairy sealskin 4 cm broad which is folded. Inside the mitten there are remains of an inner mitten of birdskin, sewn on at the wrist together with the strip of sealskin. Some baleen wool was also found inside.

Buttons and buckles. — L3:12553 is a 4 cm long seal phalanx with a transverse hole, presumably used as a toggle-shaped button. — L3:12106 is a buckle of walrus ivory, 1.8 cm long, made in the shape of a figure 8. — Four buttons of walrus ivory rounded and having a curved hole on the inner side like that in I. Pl. 37.23 were also found. L3:12273 is T-shaped in cross-section, similar to those seen in I. Pl. 37.25. The object seen on Pl. 1.7 is a small, toggle-shaped button of walrus ivory, of flattened V-shape, each end carved into an animal head, most likely a bear's head. — Two specimens, L3:12595 and 12754, are pieces of walrus ivory, 2.4 and 2.2 cm long, with a longitudinally drilled hole. Possibly they are unfinished tubular buttons, or the like.

A small *bead of amber*, L3:13176, of irregular shape, resembling that shown in I. Pl. 37.28 was found.

Tooth pendants. — Nine bears' canine teeth having a suspension hole through the root end. Of these, L3:12426 has the hole bored obliquely from one side to the end. On L3:12159 the hole is oblong, and made by cutting. Seven of the specimens have been flaked at the fore-end, and on at least two of these, L3:12859 and 13206, the edges have again become rounded by wear, possibly through use as flint flakers.

Four pendants of fox canines resembling that in I. Pl. 38.25. Seventy one tiny incisors, lengths 1.1—1.5 cm, with a small hole drilled through the root end, were found together in house 20 in addition to one longer canine tooth.

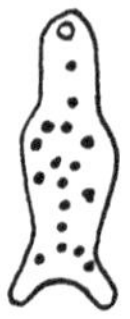

Fig. 60. Pendant with dot ornament, from Nûgdlît house 28.

Pendants. — L3:12320 is a drop pendant of soapstone, 4 cm long and 1.5 cm broad at the base. It has two transverse, ornamental grooves. The upper end is sharply wedge-shaped with a transverse hole. — L3:12457 is made from a white whale tooth of which the top has been rounded; its size is 3.8 × 1 cm. — One flat pendant, shown on Pl. 1.17, is made of walrus ivory. L3:12861, fig. 60, is also of walrus ivory, 2.9 × 1.1 cm, rather crudely made. In the middle of one side is an ornamental dot. On the other side is a dot ornament as shown on the figure.

The *chain pendant* seen on Pl. 1.10 is one of two identical specimens made of walrus ivory.

Pl. 1.12 is a peculiar, spherical piece of walrus ivory with four slanting 'legs', of which two are broken. Possibly also the two preserved 'legs' were originally longer. Use unknown.

Snowbeaters of baleen. — Ten specimens, of which four are complete, lengths 34—56 cm. The handles are waisted, an on three of the specimens have a bilateral extension at the end, almost as in I. Pl. 45.11. On L3:12176, which is 36 cm long, there are two large notches opposite one another, presumably for suspension by a strap.

In addition to the objects made of skin described above, 20 fragments of *worked skin* were found, as well as five fragments of *skin thongs* and two pieces of *plaited sinew thread*.

Games and toys.

Ajagaq. — Only one ajagaq was found, L3:12461. It is made from the humerus of a seal (cf. I. Pl. 39.1). In the middle are marks made by a string which was originally tied on. — L3:12037 is most likely an *ajagaq stick* of wood, 10.2 × 1.2 cm, with a groove roughly in the middle. One end is rounded, the other somewhat flattened.

Two oval *top disks* made of baleen, like that shown in I. Pl. 48.11 were found. On one specimen there are three holes in addition to the central one.

Fifteen *gambling bones* of seal phalanges resembling those in I. Pl. 39.22-23 were found.

Carved animal figures. — Pl. 1.16 is a dog figure of walrus ivory. L3:12594 is a 7 cm long figure, presumably also representing a dog, crudely made from a flat piece of walrus ivory. Furthermore, an unfinished bear figure was found, and Pl. 1.8 is a peculiar little figure of walrus ivory. — A '*swimming bird*' of walrus ivory, L3:13144, 4.2 cm long was found. It has a suspension hole in the rear, and, on the back side of the neck, three ornamental dots, one behind the other.

Dolls. — In addition to a fragment only two small, crudely made wooden dolls were found, (L3:12737); lengths 3.6 and 3.2 cm. No doubt they are meant to represent a man and his wife, since they were found tied close together with baleen string.

Three specimens of *bird bones stuck one into another* with lengths varying from 10.7 to 17 cm. — A *feather quill*, 32 cm long, with only a small tuft left at the end, had most likely been used as a toy dart. — A *toy harpoon*, L3:12745, 15.5 cm long, was also found. It is made from one piece of wood, the foreshaft and a broad socket piece being indicated.—

Pl. 2.8 is a *toy weapon of baleen* with a barbed point, the butt ending in a curved point, no doubt representing an ice pick. — L3:12887 is the broken fore-end of a *toy leister* of baleen, or some such object. — L3:12771 is the end piece of a very small wooden, *toy bow*, and L3:12744 is a *toy arrow*, resembling that in I. Pl. 41.28. It is about 21 cm long and composed of two pieces. L3:12741 is a similar arrow but only 9 cm long. L3:12365 is a toy baleen arrow, 12.5 cm long, with a blade and a long barb. Of three butts of *toy arrow shafts* two have the flat rear end extremely widened. — L3:12522 is the fore end of a *toy sling handle* of wood.

One *cross slat of a toy sledge*, (L3:13108), made of wood; length 9 cm, breadth 1.2 cm was found. The ends are tapered as in I. Pl. 41.5. — L3:12857 is a fragment of a hollowed-out *toy umiaq*. The ends are damaged, but as far as can be seen they were without the characteristic horns, the shape thus corresponding to that in I. Pl. 42.2-3. L3:12746 is presumably the blade end of a *toy umiaq oar*. Its maximum breadth, about 2 cm, is at the end, which has the corners rounded, the breadth decreasing rapidly at the transition to the shaft. — L3:12620 is a solid *toy kayak* of wood, 14.6 × 1.9 × 1 cm. The upper side is almost plane, the bottom flat. The stem is sharp and a little higher than the more evenly tapering stern.

A *toy snow knife* made of baleen, 11.5 cm long, a little curved and having an oblong hole for a handle in the broad rear end. In type it resembles that shown in I. Pl. 18.2. — Three crudely made soapstone *toy lamps* of no typical form were also found, as well as a *toy pot*, (L3:12508), elongated oval in shape, 5.8 × 3.8 × 2 cm, and resembling that in I. Pl. 43.21. Two other fragments are of similar pots.

Objects associated with intellectual culture.

Drum[1]). — One fragment of a drum (L3:12296) was found. The frame which is made of baleen, is 3 cm broad, with a deep groove in the outer side. Where the two ends of the frame overlap, a handle of wood, 8.5 cm long, is tied on with a baleen cord. The inner one of the two overlapping pieces is here a little broader than the other, and a notch has been cut in it to fit the handle. The inner half of the handle, i. e. the part next to the frame, is almost wedge-shaped, with a flat upper side without a groove for the frame. On the opposite side there are two transversal grooves for a lashing.

---

[1]) I was told in 1946 that the purpose of the peculiar carved edge seen on several bone drum frames (shown in I. fig. 102.1-4) is only to improve the sound of the drum.

Amulet. — L3:12466 is a small pack of unknown contents with a skin wrapping, tied round with a broad strip of sinews. It can hardly be anything but an amulet. — L3:13050 is a small *amulet box* of wood, 3.1 × 1.5 cm, with one compartment, resembling that in I. Pl. 39.21.

Unidentified objects.

About 180 more or less worked pieces of bone or similar material, including unidentifiable fragments of artefacts were found in addition to 95 pieces of wood, 42 pieces of baleen, and several pieces of baleen

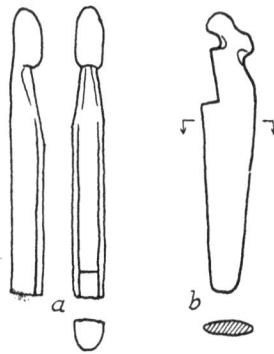

Fig. 61. Unidentified objects from Nûgdlît.

strips and lines with knots. Only a few of these specimens deserve particular notice.

Pl. 2.6 is a broad blade of bone, a little curved longitudinally. Its length is 12.5 cm, the thickness 0.4—0.5 cm. A piece is broken off at one side but seems once to have been lashed to it, the total breadth of the fore-end thus becoming about 11 cm, of the rear about 9 cm. The fore-edge is rounded by wear, as if it had been used as a shovel—or maybe as a skin scraper. The holes in the rear suggest that a broad handle had been attached, thus making its use as a scraper most probable.

L3:12280, fig. 61.a, is part of a broken stick of walrus ivory. The piece is 5.6 cm long and 0.6 cm thick, almost round, but with one side flattened. At the end a rounded 'head' has been made by cutting in from the flat side. An ornamental line runs along both edges of the flat side; the two lines being in one place connected by a single cross-line. Along each of the adjacent sides runs a similar longitudinal line.

L3:12584, fig. 61.b, resembles in shape a barb for a salmon spear. It is made of bone, 5.5 cm long, with a flat oval cross-section. At the rear end it has a plain cut and two lashing notches. The fore end seems to be rounded by wear.

L3:12953 is a heavy ring of baleen, about 25 × 25 cm, made of a long strip of baleen rolled up three times. Inside, the breadth of the strip is 5 cm, decreasing outwards. In one place is the remainder of a baleen cord tying.

L3:12794 is a segment-shaped ring, 29 × 19 cm, made of a 4.5 cm broad strip of baleen, jointed with the ends overlapping 18 cm on the

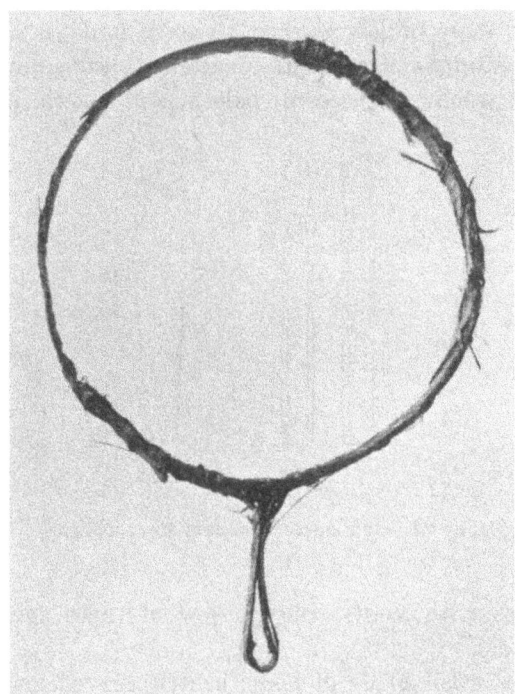

Fig. 62. Baleen ring of unknown use. Nûgdlît house 26.

straight side. In each of the four sharp corners there is a hole at the edge, and at a distance of 4 cm from these there are corresponding pairs of holes, both in the straight and the convex side. At the end of the outer part of the strip is a broad whipping of baleen strips. The overlapping ends are only kept together by a cord which is fastened through one of the holes at the corners, then slung four times around the side, and tied in the hole in the opposite edge of the other corner. — The object may have served as a lamp stand.

L3:12796, fig. 62, is a ring, about 25 cm in diameter, made of a baleen strip 1.3—2 cm broad, part of which has been bent so as to form a handle about 10 cm long. — L3:12372 is a similar but smaller ring, about 15 cm in diameter, and with a 5 cm long handle.

L3:12141 is a 20 cm long fragment of a baleen strip one centimeter broad with the remains of a loose netting of baleen cord.

Four pieces of *flint refuse* were found, besides a piece of *rock crystal* and three pieces of *mica*. — Twenty-three unidentifiable or unworked pieces of *iron*, all small and corroded by rust were also found. All of them seem to be of meteoric iron. — In six houses cut *human hair* was found.

The cultural and chronological position of Nûgdlît.

As has already been mentioned, Nûgdlît very soon gave the impression of having strong affinities to the so-called Ruinø phase of the Thule culture, which exhibits a certain western character. The impression was founded, primarily, upon the particular arrangement of the houses, with interior fire-places; secondly upon the peculiar harpoon heads with a knob on the spur. A general view of all the finds confirms this immediate impression, but at the same time it is evident that Nûgdlît, in certain respects, differs from the Ruinø. To elucidate this, and in order to make a more exact judgement of the cultural and chronological position of Nûgdlît, it will be necessary to make a special analysis of the finds.

A comparison of types found at Nûgdlît with those from the remaining part of the Thule district gives the following result, (cf. the table in Part II. pp. 42—59).

Found solely at Nûgdlît:
    House with anteroom.
    Summer dwelling, partly subterranean.
    Richly ornamented harpoon head (Pl. 1.1).
    Swivel with three "windows" (Pl. 1.9).
    Small socket piece with scarf.
    Plug for towing bladder (?) (Pl. 1.21).
    Sinew twister of walrus ivory.
    Leister-harpoon head of baleen (Pl. 1.22).
    Toboggan (?) (fig. 40).
    Umiaq cover.
    Harpoon rest for umiaq (fig. 43).
    Boat-hook (fig. 44).
    Broad end mounting for kayak paddle.
    Snow knife handle with a bed for the blade (Pl. 2.5).
    Simple knife with side-blade.
    Spatula-shaped baleen knife (Pl. 2.7).
    Chopping block of whale vertebra.
    Ground side-scraper of flint (Pl. 1.20).
    Segment-shaped ulo handle (Pl. 2.1).
    Urine scraper of walrus ivory.
    Fish spoon (?) of baleen (Pl. 2.4).
    Gutskin jacket with flaps.
    Birdskin hood.
    Birdskin trousers.

Stocking.
Buckle, 8-shaped.
"Swimming bird".
Bird bones stuck one into another.
Toy weapon of bird quill.
Toy umiaq oar blade.
Toy snow knife with handle hole.

Altogether 31 types, or 17 % of the total number of 186.

Nûgdlît and Ruinø only:

Qagsse (ceremonial house).
Line buckle, bear's head.
Line buckle, bear figure.
Sledge runner of walrus ivory.
Pick-axe head.
Birdskin jacket.
Amulet bundle.

In all, 7 types, or about 3.8 %. — If to these we add the group *Thule-e*, which culturally proved to be closely associated with the Ruinø, we get further:

Harpoon head Thule-2 with knob on the spur.
Harpoon head Thule-3 with knob on the spur.
Stopper for harpoon line with spike in the middle.
"Winged" pendant.

This gives in all 11 types, or 6 %.

Nûgdlît, Thule culture and Dorset only:

Small mending plug.
Cylindrical socket-piece.
Bow brace of baleen (cf. I. Pl. 47.7).
Hatchet head of walrus tusk (Dorset).
(Mattock handle).
Fat scraper with straight edge.
(Thimble).
Bone hook.
(Mitten).
Button of seal phalanx (I. Pl. 37.26).
"Winged" button.
Bead of amber.
Toy arrow of baleen.

In all, 10 types, or 5.4 %; the types placed within brackets not being counted, as it is obviously due to accident that they do not appear in finds from the later periods.

Nûgdlît and the Inugsuk phase only:

Sealing stool leg, of wood.
Flint flaker of rib.

Pointed caribou ulna.
Blubber fork of wood.
Tube-shaped button.
Toy harpoon of wood.
Toy lamp, no ledge.

In all, 7 types, or 3.8 %.

Nûgdlît, Ruinø group, Thule culture, and Dorset only:
Arrow heads with tang with a raised ridge.
Knife handle of two halves.
Flint flaker of walrus ivory.
(Needle of bone).
Ladle of musk-ox horn.
Bear figure.

In all, 5 types, or 2.2 %.

Nûgdlît, Ruinø group, and Inugsuk phase only:
House with a kitchen.
Kayak deck beam (?) of bone.
Adze head, no holes.
Adze head, vertical holes.
Adze handle with three holes.
Blubber fork of baleen.
Bone button with ventral hole.
Toy dart of baleen with many barbs.

In all, 8 types, or 4.3 %.

As the group Thule-d holds an important position for attempts to estimate the relation to the older culture, it will be natural also to examine the types in common only with this group.

Nûgdlît, Thule-d, and one or more of the Ruinø group, Thule culture, and Dorset:
Harpoon head Thule-2, common type.
Lance head with rest for a blade.
Bone plug with head.
Snow shovel of bone.
Stone maul head (Thule-d and Ruinø).
Adze head, horizontal holes.
Flint flaker of walrus penis bone.
Flint flaker of antler.
Convex flint scraper.
Two-handed scraper of walrus penis bone (Thule-d).
Pottery (Thule-d and Ruinø).
Blubber fork of bone.
Pendant of bone.
Chain ornament.

In all, 14 types, or about 7.5 %.

In a similar way those types can be enumerated which are only found to the depth of the more recent period of Thule culture, which, to a certain extent bears the Inugsuk character, the so-called "early transitional". Thus we get

Nûgdlît, Inugsuk, Ruinø group, and early transitional:
    Toggle with oblong hole.
    Trace buckle, holes at right angles.
    Baleen knife.
    Drill shank of bone.
    Adze handle, one hole.
    Cup-shaped scraper.
    Bodkin.
    Lamp, no ledge.
    Oval bottom of baleen.
    Laddle of wood.
    Edge mounting.
    (Boot).
    Ajagaq, seal humerus.
    Top disk of baleen.
    Bow of wood.
    Toy kayak.
    Toy umiaq.
    Toy pot, oval.

In all, 17 types, or 9 %.

If the percentages thus computed are grouped according to the chronological periods of which they are representative, we get the following scheme:

Inugsuk	Thule-e	Ruinø group	early tr.	Thule	Dorset	Nûgdlît spec.
3.8		6	5.4			17
	4.3		2.2			
			7.5			
	9					
		44.8				
In all: 17		45	15			

As the (approximately) 45 % of types found in all the culture groups are af no chronological importance, only elucidating their mutual cultural background; and as the 17 % and the 15 %, which display affinities to more recent and older periods respectively almost cancel one another out, the percentage of specific likeness to the Ruinø group becomes decisive. When examining the chronological position of the Ruinø group (see II. p. 73), the percentages of more recent and older affinities respectively, were 13.5 % and 12 %, thus, just as at Nûgdlît, suggesting a slight displacement towards the Inugsuk period. As far as such statistical calculation go, it appears that Nûgdlît must be placed in the same period as the Ruinø group.

If only those figures which indicate the specific likeness to Inugsuk, Ruinø group, and Thule culture respectively are taken into consideration, one might be inclined to place Nûgdlît a little more towards the last one, but this is, in part, outweighed by the number of types of a wider distribution which point to a more recent date. Moreover, if the actual types are considered, it becomes evident that the common characteristics of Nûgdlît and the Ruinø group far outweigh the specific likeness to the Thule culture.

Bearing, as they do, a relatively great resemblance to one another, the two groups have a correspondingly alien character when compared with the local culture of the Thule district. The Ruinø group showed 16.5 per cent of special elements, which nearly corresponds to the 17 per cent of Nûgdlît. Here, however, it must be borne in mind that the material used for the comparison with Nûgdlît includes the type inventory of the Ruinø group, and, as the elements common to just these two groups belong to the special features of the Ruinø group, Nûgdlît will appear still more alien.

In spite of the great mutual similarity, it appears that the two groups do not represent exactly the same cultural level. The Ruinø phase, as it appears to us, conveys the impression that a certain adaptation to new surroundings had already taken place in the Thule district—if not farther to the west. Nothing can yet be said for certain about this, since only little is known so far about the archaeology of Ellesmere Island and the arctic archipelago. On some of the few fragments of arrow heads from the Ruinø phase the tang has the knobs characteristic of the Thule culture, and the Ruinø people had acquired some Norse objects. Further, they had also had connections with a culture of a Dorset character. On Nûgdlît, on the other hand, no Norse objects were found; nothing, except maybe the ground flint scraper (Pl. 1.20), indicates a connection with Dorset culture, and all the arrow heads found have the western type of tang with a raised ridge. Even if both Nûgdlît and the Ruinø group bear a western stamp, it is clear that this more particularly applies to Nûgdlît.

As to the chronological position of Nûgdlît, judged from a greenlandic point of view, two possibilities may be considered:

1) Nûgdlît may have been inhabited by the same group of people which we later find on the Ruinø, where an adaptation to the local culture had to some extent taken place. If this be the case, Nûgdlît in all probability belongs to the beginning of the 14th, or maybe the end of the 13th century.

2) Nûgdlît represents an independent, 'fresh' immigration, at a juncture which cannot be ascertained with certainty, but which, due to the cultural likeness to the Ruinø phase, must be assumed to have taken place most probably also within the 13th—14th centuries.

Comparative remarks.

As the former special traits of the Ruinø group have been discussed in Part II, p. 149 ff., only a few remarks will be given here on the new traits from Nûgdlît.

It can be assumed that it is merely due to chance that some of the 31 types mentioned on p. 95 f., which, within the Thule district, have only been found at Nûgdlît, were not found elsewhere in the district, while others are of little value for comparative investigation. This may be said of the umiaq cover, the sinew twister made of walrus ivory (cf. that of I. Pl. 10.12, made of wood), the simple knife with sideblade, the chopping block of whale vertebra, the toy weapon of bird quill, and the toy umiaq oar blade.

With regard to the identifiable pieces of garments, to which I shall revert later, the matter is more difficult, since we lack sufficient material from this early period for comparison, and, in particular, since we have no direct knowledge of the cut of the garments used in those times. Even if it can be taken for granted that people elsewhere in Greenland have used e. g. gutskin jackets, yet they may have been of another type.

Some of the types are known from the central Thule culture. This is true of the toboggan[1]), the snow knife handle with a bed for the blade[2]), the segment-shaped ulo handle[3]), the "swimming bird"[4]), and the bird bones stuck one into another[5]). — A snow knife with a handle hole for actual use has been found in Inglefield Land (I. Pl. 18.1-2). The small socket piece with a scarf presumably also belongs to the central and eastern Thule culture, where socket pieces with a scarf are common in large harpoons.

The only specimen which, with any degree of certainty, could be assumed to be a connecting link with the Dorset culture is the ground side-scraper of flint. "A chipped and ground chert tool of uncertain purpose" is recorded by Rowley[6]). As far as can be judged from the illustration, it resembles the specimen from Nûgdlît.

---

[1]) Th. Mathiassen 1927, I. p. 45; II. p. 62.
[2]) Ibid. I. Pl. 15.9.
[3]) Ibid. I. Pl. 23.5.
[4]) Ibid. I. Pl. 321-5.
[5]) Ibid. I. Pl. 52.10.
[6]) G. Rowley 1940, p. 495, fig. 2g.

It is true that a few of the remaining types somewhat resemble others known in Greenland, but their occurrence there must be supposed to be secondary in relation to Nûgdlît and the Ruinø group. Indeed, it seems likely that they had been introduced there by these groups. In particular this holds good of the broad end mounting for a kayak oar, which corresponds to an oar with a slender blade, commonly used in Greenland today. The kayak oar of the Thule culture usually had a rather wide, pointed lanceolate blade resembling the type commonly used outside Greenland, as assumed by Mathiassen[1]). This assumption is supported by the finds from the Thule district. Certainly, kayak oars with rather slender blades are not quite unknown among the Central Eskimos, but they differ from the Greenland type in having the ends pointed or rounded. Only in connection with Copper Eskimos are rectangularly shaped oar blades mentioned[2]).

Harpoon line *swivels* of various forms are known from Baffin Island[3]), and from archaeological finds from Greenland. The barrel-shape, however, is best known from Northeast Greenland[4]) and Thule (I. p. 195). Yet, none of these are of the particular Nûgdlît type with three 'windows', which bear a certain likeness to swivels from Ipiutak; although the latter, it is true, have only two large openings[5]).

Boat-hooks are said to have been in use in West Greenland in former times[6]), and a wooden handle found at Kangâmiut by Mathiassen seems to have been fitted with a lashed-on barb of a shape similar to that from Nûgdlît[7]). Hooks of this type are common in Alaska, being used both as boat-hooks and blubber hooks, and known from such early finds as those from Punuk and Old Bering Sea[8]), whereas in Greenland blubber hooks were of another type, with an inset barb[9]).

Urine scrapers made of the root end of a walrus tusk are still known in the Thule district.

Two small plugs with a line-hole (p. 65) have tentatively been listed as plugs for towing bladders. Their particular shape with the narrow, protruding collar indicates that they were inserted in a bladder or skin. The possibility cannot be excluded, however, that they are buckles for some kind of skin garment. To a certain extent they resemble the specimen, (a 'line-buckle'), shown in I. Pl. 38.6, the actual use of

---

[1]) Th. Mathiassen 1930, p. 208.
[2]) K. Birket-Smith 1945, p. 188.
[3]) Fr. Boas 1901, p. 36, fig. 45.
[4]) H. Larsen 1934, Pl. 2.16; S. Richter 1934, fig. 85.7; P. V. Glob 1935, p. 48.
[5]) H. Larsen and Fr. Rainey 1948, Pl. 56, 57.
[6]) K. Birket-Smith 1924, p. 260.
[7]) Th. Mathiassen 1931, p. 109, fig. 37.
[8]) H. B. Collins 1937, p. 138 f.
[9]) K. Birket-Smith 1924, p. 390, fig. 287.

which has not yet been ascertained. The likeness to a 'unique specimen of problematic use', figured by Geist and Rainey[1]) is still greater, the latter only differing from the Nûgdlît specimen shown on Pl. 1.21 in being partly wedge-shaped. Possibly all the specimens mentioned have been of similar use.

A harpoon rest for an umiaq (fig. 43) is only known in Alaska, where it dates back to Punuk times[2]).

The harpoon head, Pl. 1.1, is of a shape which is characteristic of several harpoon heads from the Ruinø phase, but a specimen with a similar, elaborate ornamentation has not been found before. The Y-ornament and the spur-lines have an obvious Thule character, but the line pattern and the cross ornament bear an alien stamp. Considering the style in general, and the application of a curved spur-line in front of the linehole in particular, the ornamentation to some extent resembles that of a harpoon head recorded by Geist and Rainey and classed as "Rare type 10"[3]). It was found $12^1/_2$ feet below the surface, corresponding to Punuk-Birnirk layers. The curved spur-line and the cross ornament are both a common Ipiutak form[4]). The cross is also found in Dorset and in recent Alaska ornamentations[5]), but it seems to be unknown in the central Thule culture.

The leister harpoon head of baleen, Pl. 1.22, had presumably been used for fishing. Apart from the material of which it is made it closely resembles a point for a fish spear from Alaska, recorded by Nelson[6]). No doubt such harpoon heads are closely related to old types of bladder dart heads, and if made of bone or ivory, they can often hardly be distinguished in archaeological finds.

The spatula-shaped baleen knife, Pl. 2.7, and baleen "fish spoon", Pl. 2.4, seem to be unique, as is apparently also the 8-shaped buckle (p. 90).

The winter houses at Nûgdlît correspond in all essentials to types already known from the Thule district as described in Part I. A new feature is the solidly built anteroom in front of house 23 (fig. 20). Similar anterooms, built, however, of wooden logs, are common in houses in Alaska, but they have not hitherto been found in Greenland, where they seem to have been abandoned early on, as was apparently the case with several other peculiarities of the Ruinø people.

---

[1]) O. W. Geist and Fr. Rainey 1936, Pl. 54.33; p. 159.

[2]) H. B. Collins 1937, Pl. 79.10.

[3]) O. W. Geist and Fr. Rainey 1936, p. 180, fig. 29. Cf. also p. 202, fig. 33.

[4]) See f. i. H. Larsen and Fr. Rainey 1948, figs. 13, 41, 43.

[5]) E. W. Nelson 1899, Pl. LXVI.4; W. Hoffman 1897, Pl. 32.1, 34.2, 68, figs. 105, 134.

[6]) E. W. Nelson 1899, Pl. LXVIII.29. See also L. Giddings 1952, Pl. XXVIII.3, "Salmon harpoon head", from Ekseavik.

Roof supports generally consisting of wooden posts erected along the edge of the sleeping platform were a common trait in later communal houses in Greenland. But it would seem as if the high, apparently detached stone pillars seen in house 30 (figs. 28, 29) had a more particular relation to the roof supports of the western, four-post houses. Its extraordinary dimensions and the absence of sleeping platforms indicate that house 30 was a qagsse. In that case it is not surprising that an otherwise abandoned building custom had been maintained, though adapted to the material at hand.

Ruins of partly subterranean summer dwellings such as those found at Nûgdlît have not been described before, as far as I know. Unfortunately nothing was left to indicate their exact dimensions, or to give a hint as to what their structure as a whole was like. One may only guess that they had some resemblance to the oval, Siberian Eskimo dwellings which are covered with walrus hide.

It is of special interest that the finds from Nûgdlît include fairly well preserved pieces of garments, which in the case of the gutskin jackets have even made it possible to ascertain the cut. Unfortunately only one specimen (fig. 49—50) is complete enough for the shape of the lower part to be seen. The large flaps in the front and back suggest, in this case, that the jacket had not been meant for kayak use. It may be a woman's jacket, but on the other hand it is not unlikely that gutskin jackets of this shape had also been worn by men. All the gutskin jackets in the Ethnographical Collection of the National Museum in Copenhagen have a horizontal, straight-cut lower edge, with the exception of one specimen (c. 376): a little girl's jacket from Southeast Greenland with small flaps of equal lengths, but in other respects not resembling the Nûgdlît jackets. Further, Hatt has described a gutskin jacket from the Yukon area in Alaska, which ends, front and back, in a rounded flap[1]).

Here it might be worth mentioning, that the gutskin jacket is not unknown to the Polar Eskimos, as hitherto generally assumed, even if it has gone out of use in recent years. During my stay there I was told that most of the women still know how to sew a "kapiseq", and a man who was still alive had worn such a jacket. It was made of intestines of the barbed seal, and the cut "resembled that of a cotton wool ánorâq". Of course this is a rather vague statement, and unfortunately I failed to ascertain the exact cut. In addition they gave me the information, that gutskin jackets "were not used in kayaks, but only as overclothing". Here it must be borne in mind that the construction of a kayak had also been forgotten by the Polar Eskimos through a period of uncertain

---

[1]) Hatt 1914, p. 115.

length, but, nevertheless, the information about the gutskin jacket may be in accordance with an old tradition, all the more so as gutskin jackets have been used in the same way in recent times in East Greenland.

The few facts mentioned above suggest that a gutskin jacket with long flaps, resembling those on ordinary skin coats, once belonged to the dress of the eskimos from the arctic coast—maybe even before the special kayak jacket was developed, and, perhaps, having some connection with the predominating umiaq hunting of the western eskimos.

As shown on p. 81, the Nûgdlît gutskin jackets are characteristic in being "built up" starting from the hood, the "supporting" part being formed by the hood-and-shoulder yoke, with front strips which continue right down the body, which is also made of vertical strips. An investigation of the gutskin jackets in the National Museum has proved that exactly the same principle is still used in recent jackets from Pt. Hope (Mus. nr. P. 6503), East Cape, Siberia (P. 32.7), and St. Lawrence Island (P. 1675). The cut of these jackets only deviates little from that of the Nûgdlît ones, the main difference being that the yoke of the former reaches right out to the sleeve seams, whereas on the latter a strip on each side passes above the shoulder from front to back, between the distal end of the yoke and the sleeve seam. This, no doubt, must be taken as a trait pointing to the general eastern type, the main characteristic of which is the fact that all the strips of the body, except the central ones, pass above the shoulder, thus omitting the shoulder yoke. The western jackets mentioned also lack the triangular chin piece, instead of which a whole strip has been inserted, reaching from the chin down to the lower edge, thus forming the central front strip of the body. On the other hand they have kept the inset gores in the upper parts of the breast and the back. Also the strip which extends out from the side of the body to the under side of the sleeve, ending in a gore, has been preserved in principle. The only difference is that the western jackets have no continuous strip, but the sleeve part consists of two gores sewn together, which have themselves been sewn to the upper end of the side strip of the body.

This method of strengthening the connection between body and sleeve has been carried through completely in men's gutskin jackets from East Greenland (f. i. Ld. 16), the side strip here continuing through the under side of the sleeve to the wristband, as already pointed out by Hatt. In other respects, however, these East Greenland jackets conform to the eastern type, the hood also being sewn on with wedge-shaped "hood yokes" extending down the front and back[1]). However, in a few gutskin jackets (Ld. 14 and one without number), which possibly

---

[1]) Hatt 1914, p. 111; Pl. IX.4.

are women's jackets, no such "hood yokes" are found, the strips forming the sides of the hood extending right down through the body in both front and back. The front part of the hood thus resembles the corresponding part of the western jackets, only the yoke is lacking, and the principle used in the front has been applied also in the back side. Thus in this case a special development of one of the original traits seems to have taken place, at the same time displaying a logical development of the "vertical" principle. As expressed by Hatt, the "hood yokes" in these jackets, as also in a jacket from Labrador, are continued down through the body[1]), but in view of the Nûgdlît finds it may now seem reasonable to look upon the shorter, wedge-shaped "hood yokes" in some of the Greenland gutskin jackets as reduced "hood yokes", originating from an old, well developed cut; although Hatt is certainly right when he assumes that this development had been influenced by the more generally adopted, or in some instances modern cut, as e. g. in West Greenland.

In Alaska, from Norton Sound southwards, the gutskin jackets are in most cases made of horizontal strips, and a "yoke" is often seen continuing from the hood and shoulder down the upper side of the sleeve right to the wristband (f. i. P. 1353, from the north side of the Yukon delta, and P. 33.1, from Nunivak). In most other respects they differ considerably from the northern type.

As the various traits which in the Nûgdlît gutskin jacket form a unit are met with almost unchanged in North Alaska and the Bering Strait area and can further be traced, more or less separately, in other places in connection with what appears to be more recent cuts, it seems likely that the Nûgdlît gutskin jackets represent in all essentials a basic type connected with the old neo-Eskimo arctic whale-hunting culture. Yet, the Nûgdlît jacket hardly displays the very oldest form. As already mentioned, the strip next to the sleeve seems to be the forerunner of a more recent development and the horizontal strips which, on two of the jackets, fill out the back of the hood (figs. 50, 52) prove that the "horizontal" principle had also been known. The latter has not developed further in the eastern area, where the back of the hood in almost all cases is also seen to be made of one broad, vertical strip, continuing down along the back of the body.

The hood-and-shoulder yoke, as used in gutskin jackets, has apparently not been applied to any large extent in jackets made from hairy skins. It can, however, still be seen in the white "aterdlak" of the Polar Eskimo men's foxskin jacket, which again indicates a close connection of this particular cut with the Thule culture.

---

[1]) Hatt 1914, p. 111 f.

The general impression conveyed by this short survey only supports the assumption arrived at through the more detailed analysis in Part II, that the people of the Ruinø phase were immigrants who, within a rather limited period, made their way eastward from Alaska, but not as the first carriers of the Thule culture. No doubt they formed a secondary wave, carrying with them their original culture of western character. The ornamentation and the frequent occurrence of rudimentary spurs on harpoon heads, in particular together with a series of features mentioned in Part II. p. 148 ff., suggest that the Ruinø phase belongs mainly to the "Western Thule", as described by Larsen and Rainey[1]). Thus far the Ruinø and Nûgdlît finds may add to the general picture of this culture phase, a more thorough investigation of which is still to be desired, and safe conclusions as to their closer relationship and their relative chronology will only be possible if a phase, similar in details, is found in Alaska.

---

[1]) H. Larsen and Fr. Rainey 1948, p. 170 ff.

II. COMER'S MIDDEN

During the excavations in 1937, which have been described in Pt. I. p. 144 ff., the barren ground was not reached in the two innermost rows of squares: (16—13—14—18—21 and 20—19—22). The work was therefore continued here in August and September 1946, the excavation field being extended to a new row of 2 × 2 m squares towards the east and a further two metres towards the north. The bulk of the material found in 1946 thus originates from the northeastern corner of the midden, where the thickness reached a maximum of a little more than one meter. The division into "layers" has been based upon the daily levellings of the removed thawed layers, and in all essentials corresponds to that used in 1937.

In the new part of the excavation field several stones were found, no doubt originally belonging to houses which had been situated beyond, on top of the midden. No definite ground plan could be ascertained in the excavated area. Apparently the midden still extends some distance towards the east, but here conditions for excavating work are difficult, the stratification becoming blurred by the presence of disturbed houses. Midden layers are also found towards the north, but nothing can be said with certainty regarding their thickness, because the surface slopes rather much, and the rock forming the bottom may be very uneven. In the spring of 1947 some test squares were started in this place but were abandoned soon after on account of the trip to Nûgdlît, the result thus only being a collection of recent finds from the top layer.

In the following list of specimens an asterisk indicates that the type in question had not hitherto been found in Comer's midden. Thus, of the 37 types found, the tension piece for a harpoon line, the swivel, the mouth-piece for towing bladder, the ferrule for a whip shank, the lamp with no ledge, and the toy bow of bone are apparently of recent date; whereas the harpoon head of the main Thule-2 type, but with a blade at right angles to the linehole and *slots*, the baleen catcher, the fish hook of special type, the two-handed scraper of antler, and the toy sealing stool seat have not been found in the Thule district before. These few elements, however, make no change in the general picture arrived at from previous finds.

Table 2. List of specimens from Comer's midden, 1947.

	Ref. page:	Layer 1	Layer 2	Layer 3	Layer 4	Layer 5	Layer 6	Layer 7	Layer 8
Harpoon head, thin, open socket:									
* Thule-2, lashing holes	112	..	..	..	..	..	..	1	..
* Two barbs, blade ⊥ linehole, slots	—	..	..	..	..	..	..	..	1
— — — holes	—	..	..	..	..	..	..	1	1
— unfinished	—	..	..	..	..	..	..	..	1
Thule-1, lashing holes	—	..	1	1	..	..	..	..	..
Thule-3, — —	—	..	2	2	..	2	2	..	..
Harpoon head, thin, closed socket:									
Inugsuk type	113	..	..	1	1	1	1	2	1
* Long dorsal spur, blade ⊥ linehole	—	..	..	..	..	..	..	..	1
*Tension piece for harpoon line, modern type	Pl. 4.8	1	..	..	..	..	..	..	..
*Swivel, late type	Pl. 4.3	1	..	..	..	..	..	..	..
*Mouth-piece for towing bladder	Pl. 4.1-2	2	..	..	..	..	..	..	..
Plug for mouth-piece	113	..	..	..	..	..	..	2	..
Oval mending disc, wood	—	..	1	..	..	1	2	..	?
— — — baleen	114	..	..	..	..	..	1	..	..
Foreshaft for ice-hunting harpoon	—	1	3	8	5	1	1	3	..
Socket-piece for harpoon, cylindrical	—	..	2	2	..	..	..	..	..
Finger rest	—	1	..	..	1	..	..	..	..
*Harpoon rest (?), baleen	—	..	..	..	..	..	..	2	..
*Lance head, movable	—	..	..	1	..	1	1	1	1
Lance blade, slate	—	..	..	1	..	..	..	..	..
Ice pick, with scarf	—	..	..	..	..	..	..	4	2
Wound pin	115	..	1	3	..	..	..	2	..
Sealing stool leg	—	..	..	..	1	1	..	2	..
Bird dart side-prong, inside barbs	—	..	..	..	..	..	..	3	..
— — fragm. butt	—	..	..	..	1	..	..	..	..
Throwing board	—	..	..	1	..	..	1	..	..
Weapon shafts of wood, fragments	—	..	..	2	4	1	2	3	..
Bow, wood	—	..	..	..	..	..	..	1	..
— antler	—	..	1	..	..	..	..	..	..
— baleen	—	..	..	1	..	1	..	2	1
Bow brace	—	..	..	..	..	..	1	2	1
Arrow head, lanceolate, unsymmetrical	116	..	..	..	..	..	..	..	1
— — symmetrical	—	..	..	2	1	..	2	2	..
— with barb	—	..	..	..	..	1	..	2	..
— fragm. of butt with knobs	—	..	..	1	..	..	..	1	..
Arrow shaft fragm.	—	..	..	4	5	4	6	5	1
Barb for salmon spear (?), with scarf	—	..	..	..	..	..	1	1	1
* — — — (?), lashing holes	—	..	1	..	..	..	..	..	..
Leister prong, bone	117	..	..	1	..	..	..	..	..
* — — baleen	Pl. 3.11	..	..	..	..	..	1	..	..
*Leister harpoon head	117	..	..	1	..	..	1	..	..

Table 2 (continued).

	Ref. page:	Layer 1	Layer 2	Layer 3	Layer 4	Layer 5	Layer 6	Layer 7	Layer 8
Trout needle, antler	117	..	..	..	1	..	..	..	..
* — — (?), baleen	132	..	..	..	1	..	1	..	..
*Baleen catcher	Fig. 63	..	..	..	..	..	..	1	..
Gull hook, oblique groove	118	..	1	..	..	..	1	3	..
*Gorge	—	..	..	..	..	..	..	..	1
*Fish hook	Pl. 3.8	..	..	..	..	..	1	..	..
*Bola	118	..	..	..	..	..	..	1	..
Toggle	—	..	..	1	1	..	..	..	..
— with oblong hole	—	..	..	..	..	..	..	1	1
Ferrule	—	..	..	..	1	1	..	..	..
Bone bolt	—	..	..	..	1	1	..	..	..
Peg of wood	119	..	..	..	5	1	5	3	..
Sledge runner (?), compound, wood, fragm.	—	1	..	..	..	..	..	..	..
Sledge shoe, bone	—	5	9	9	6	4	7	12	6
— — ivory	—	6	5	5	..	..	1	..	..
Sledge cross-slat, bone	—	..	..	..	..	..	2	2	..
— — wood	—	..	..	..	..	..	..	..	1
Trace buckle, bone	—	4	1	1	1	2	2	1	1
— — baleen	—	..	..	..	..	..	1	1	..
*Ferrule for whip shank	Pl. 4.4	1	..	..	..	..	..	..	..
Baleen stick	119	..	..	..	..	..	..	2	2
*Umiaq rib, wood	—	..	..	..	..	..	..	1	1
Harpoon rest for kayak, low	120	..	..	..	1	..	..	..	..
— — - — with foot	—	..	..	..	..	1	..	..	..
Leg for kayak rack	Pl. 4.13	..	..	..	..	..	..	..	1
Snow knife, bone	120	..	..	..	..	2	2	1	1
— — — fragment	—	..	..	1	..	3	8	5	3
Snow probe	—	..	..	..	..	..	1	..	1	..
Bone knife, blunt	—	..	1	..	..	..	..	..	..
Knife of baleen	—	..	..	..	..	..	..	1	..
Knife with end blade	—	..	..	..	2	3	3	5	2
*Knife handle of two halves	121	..	..	..	..	1	..	..	..
Flensing knife	—	..	..	..	..	..	1	..	..
Knife with side blade on one side	—	..	..	2	1	..	1	..	..
Knife with side blade on one side row of blade grooves	—	..	..	1	..	..	..	..	..
Knife with side blade on one side and end blade	—	..	..	1	..	..	1	..	1
Knife with row of blades on two sides, and end blade	—	..	..	1	..	..	..	..	..
Knife with broad blade part and narrow handle	122	..	..	..	1	..	..	..	..
Unidentifiable fragments of knife handles	—	1	1	3	1	..	4	1	1
Knife blade of slate	—	..	..	..	1	..	..	1	..
Knife of stone	—	..	..	..	..	..	..	1	..

Table 2 (continued).

Ref. page:	Layer 1	Layer 2	Layer 3	Layer 4	Layer 5	Layer 6	Layer 7	Layer 8
Ulo handle, low and thick 122	..	..	1	..	..	1	2	..
— — flat .... —	..	..	..	1	..	..	1	..
— — — trapezoidal, with hole ..... —	..	..	..	..	1	..	1	..
— — compound .... —	..	1	..	..	..	..	..	..
— modern type 123	1	..	..	..	..	..	..	..
Hand drill .... —	..	..	..	..	..	..	1	..
Bow drill shank, antler .... —	..	..	1	..	..	..	1	..
— — — wood .... —	1	1	1	1	2	..	..	..
— — mouthpiece, caribou astragalus... —	..	..	..	..	..	..	1	..
Baleen saw .... —	..	..	..	1	..	..	2	..
Stone scraper, blunt, dolomite .... —	8	13	6	4	3	10	13	..
— — with edge .... —	..	2	..	..	..	2	2	1
End scraper, bone, narrow 124	..	3	2	..	..	2	3	2
*Bone scraper, broad .... Pl. 3.3	..	..	..	..	..	1	..	..
Scraper with iron blade, modern type 124	1	..	..	..	..	..	..	..
*Two-handed scraper, antler .... Pl. 3.5	..	..	..	..	..	..	1	..
* — — bear ulna 124	..	..	..	..	..	1	..	..
Whetstone .... —	5	12	2	1	4	7	14	2
Hammer stone .... —	..	..	1	..	1	..	1	..
Adze head, no holes .... Pl. 3.2	..	..	..	..	..	..	1	..
— vertical holes 124	..	..	..	..	..	..	..	1
* — horizontal holds .... —	..	..	..	..	..	..	..	1
Bone wedge .... —	..	..	1	1	..	3	2	1
Marline spike, flat .... —	..	1	1	1	..	1	1	..
— — pointed 125	..	..	1	1	1	2	1	..
*Pointed fibula .... —	..	..	..	..	..	..	..	1
— ulna .... —	..	..	..	..	..	..	1	..
Bodkin .... —	..	1	1	1	1	1	..	..
— with ornamental rolls .... Pl. 4.11	..	..	..	..	..	1	..	..
Mattock head 125	..	..	..	..	..	2	..	..
*Cutting board, bone .... —	..	..	..	..	..	..	1	1
— — (?), baleen .... Pl. 3.12	..	..	..	..	..	..	1	..
Pyrites 125	..	3	..	..	1	3	1	..
Fire-hearth .... —	..	..	..	..	..	..	..	1
Lamp, with ledge .... —	..	..	..	1	..	1	..	..
— with low step .... —	..	..	..	1	1	..	..	..
* — modern type, no ledge .... —	1	..	..	..	..	..	..	..
— fragment .... —	1	1	1	..	1	..	..	..
* — trimmer, asbestos 126	..	1	1	..	..	..	..	..
— — wood .... —	1	1	2	6	6	23	12	4
— — — willow twig .... —	1	4	..	..	..	..	1	1
— — — for separate handle.. —	1	1	..	1	..	..	..	..
Cooking pot, fragment .... —	5	9	4	8	5	8	9	2
Soapstone bowl, fragment .... —	..	1	..	..	..	..	..	..

Table 2 (continued).

	Ref. page:	Layer 1	Layer 2	Layer 3	Layer 4	Layer 5	Layer 6	Layer 7	Layer 8
Meat tray, fragment	126	..	..	9	4	4	4	6	1
Bowl bottom, oval, wood	—	..	..	1	..	..	1	4	..
Cup — — —	—	..	..	..	..	..	1	..	..
Baleen handle	—	..	..	..	..	..	..	1	..
Tub stave	—	..	..	3	1	..	1	2	1
Wooden box, rectangular side	—	..	..	..	..	..	1	..	..
Rib for skin vessel, wood	—	..	..	..	..	2	1	..	..
Rim - — — bone	127	..	1	1	2	..	..	..	..
Edge mounting	—	..	..	1	2	..	2	1	..
Bone mounting	—	..	1	1	1	..	..	1	..
Carrying handle	—	..	1	..	..	..	..	1	..
Carrying stick (?), baleen	—	..	..	..	..	..	..	1	..
Wooden ladle, handle	—	..	..	..	1	..	..	..	..
*Sucking tube	—	..	..	..	..	..	..	..	1
Meat stick	—	1	..	..	..	..	..	1	..
Platform mat, baleen	—	..	..	1	1	1	2	2	..
Snow beater (?), bone	—	..	..	1	1	..	..	..	..
— — baleen	—	..	..	2	..	6	17	12	8
Comb, ivory	128	..	..	..	..	..	..	1	..
— baleen	Pl. 3.10	..	..	..	..	..	..	..	1
*Bead, soapstone	128	..	..	..	..	..	..	1	..
*Chain ornament	Pl. 4.5	..	..	..	..	..	1	..	..
Tooth pendant	128	..	2	..	..	..	..	1	..
— — bear tooth	—	..	..	..	..	..	1	..	..
Pendant of stone	—	..	..	..	..	1	..	..	..
Drum frame, bone	129	..	..	..	..	..	1	..	..
— handle, bone	—	..	1	..	..	..	..	..	..
Amulet box	—	..	..	..	..	..	..	1	..
— — lid	—	..	..	..	..	..	1	..	..
*Ajagaq, seal humerus	—	..	..	..	..	..	..	1	..
— — radius	—	..	1	..	1	..	..	..	..
Gambling bone, seal phalange	—	..	13	7	8	4	8	7	..
*Bear figure	—	..	..	..	1	..	..	..	..
*Dog figure	—	1	..	..	..	..	..	..	..
Doll, wood	—	..	..	..	1	..	7	2	1
— ivory	—	1	..	..	1	..	..	1	..
* — baleen	—	..	..	..	..	1	..	..	..
Top pivot	—	..	..	..	..	..	1	2	..
*Toy bow, bone	130	1	..	..	..	..	..	..	..
— arrow head, baleen	—	..	..	..	1	..	..	..	..
— — shaft	—	..	..	..	3	..	2	1	..
— sling handle, wood	—	..	..	..	..	..	1	1	..
* — sealing stool seat, wood	Pl. 3.6	..	..	..	..	..	..	1	..

Table 2 (continued).

	Ref. page:	Layer 1	Layer 2	Layer 3	Layer 4	Layer 5	Layer 6	Layer 7	Layer 8
Toy sledge runner	130	..	..	..	..	..	2	..	..
— — cross slat	—	..	4	..	1	..	..	..	..
* — ulo	—	..	..	..	..	..	1	..	..
— snow beater, baleen	—	..	..	..	1	..	..	..	..
— lamp, with ledge	—	..	..	..	1	..	..	2	..
— cooking pot	—	..	..	1	..	..	..	1	..
Unidentifiable pieces of worked soapstone	—	4	6	..	..	1	7	4	..
— — — iron	—	..	..	..	..	..	1	..	..
— — — bone	131	3	23	24	23	9	37	25	8
— — — wood	—	3	13	16	37	15	84	92	16
— — — baleen	—	..	1	3	1	1	9	10	..
Baleen lines with knobs	—	..	..	..	..	1	6	4	1
— strips	—	..	..	..	2	3	10	6	2
Objects of European origin	132	+	+	+	..	(+)	..	..	..

Description of the objects found.

Harpoon heads.

Thule-2, no blade, two pairs of holes for the lashing. — One specimen, L3:14288, was found in layer 7. It is of antler, 15.5 cm long. The socket is a little undercut and has a crudely rounded bottom.

Thule-2, blade at right angles to the line hole. — Three specimens of which L3:14730, from layer 8, is the only fairly complete one. It is of bone, 14 cm long, with *slots* for the lashing. The bottom of the socket is made by a vertical cut. At the fore-end is a hole for a plug to hold the blade. On the other two specimens L3:14521 and 14714, the butt is broken, but they can be seen to have had lashing *holes*. Both are of bone. L3:14521, from layer 7, has lost one barb, but from two lashing holes it appears that it had been repaired. At the fore-end are two plug holes for the blade. L3:14714 is from layer 8. In the same layer was also found a broken butt of an unfinished Thule-2 harpoon head of antler.

Thule-1. — Only two fragments were found, both with lashing holes. L3:13303, from layer 2, is of walrus ivory, the fore-end drilled off. L3:13506, from layer 3, is of antler.

Thule-3. — Six specimens, in addition to a small fragment and one unfinished specimen. Four of these are of antler, three of bone, and one of walrus ivory. All have lashing holes and the bottom of the socket rounded. On L3:14119, from layer 6, the lashing of baleen cord is preserved. L3:13828, from layer 5, and L3:13549 and 13548, both from layer 3, have a *dorsal* spur with an even transition from the butt end (cf. I. Pl. 4.7), whereas the others have an oblique spur. The two above-mentioned specimens from layer 3 have the fore-end widened in the plane of the blade, as seen in I. Pl. 4.14: a characteristic feature of the later forms.

Inugsuk type. — Six specimens and an unfinished one were found. Two are of walrus ivory, three of bone, and two of antler. Most of them have a broad, dorsal spur with a deep cleft, like that in I. Pl. 4.19. L3:14364 has only a small notch in the spur. L3:14712, from layer 8, is flatter in shape, almost like that in I. Pl. 4.23.

Of the type with *a closed socket, the sloping butt merging into a long dorsal spur, and a blade at right angles to the line hole*, (cf. I. Pl. 4.10), one specimen, L3:14717, was found in layer 8. It is of bone and has a plug hole for the blade. Its length is 7.8 cm.

Tension piece for harpoon line. — L3:13246, Pl. 4.8, from the uppermost layer, is a tension piece of walrus ivory. It is 5.5 cm long, 0.9—1.2 cm broad, and about 0.5 cm thick, with five holes. The fore-end is concave and has a flat groove on each side leading to the first hole. It is the type still in use.

Swivel. — One badly weathered specimen of walrus ivory, L3:13285, was found in the uppermost layer. It is shown on Pl. 4.3. It is somewhat barrel-shaped with one end tapering, but has a large opening which occupies most of one side. Its length is 3.3 cm, and greatest breadth 2 cm.

Mouth-piece for towing bladder. — Two specimens of walrus ivory, both from layer 1 were found. L3:13249, Pl. 4.1, is 5.1 cm long, almost round, but with one end somewhat flattened. In the flattened end there is a transverse hole with grooves towards the end, for attachment of a line. At the other end is a deep groove for a lashing, and an inflating hole leads obliquely from one side to the end.

L3:13248, Pl. 4.2, is heavier, and 4.5 cm long. The rear end is 2.2 cm broad, with an oval cross-section, and has a deep lashing groove. The fore end branches into two, one branch forming an extension through which a channel leads to the rear end. The other branch is flat with a hole for a line.

Two wooden *plugs for mouth-pieces*, resembling that in I. Pl. 5.20, are from layer 7.

Oval mending disc. — Four specimens of wood, resembling those in I. Pl. 5.31-32, are of the common type with a deep groove in the edge.

On L3:13996, which is 5.5 × 3 cm, the baleen lashing is preserved. — L3:14169, from layer 6, is a similar mending disc of baleen.

L3:14732, Pl. 4.6, from layer 8, may also be a mending disc. It is of wood, 2.2 × 1.8 cm, and 1.1 cm thick. Instead of a groove in the edge it has only a collar-shaped extension on one side.

Foreshafts for ice-hunting harpoon. — 22 fragments come from layers 1—7. With one exception all are of narwhal tusk with the surface ground smooth, like that shown in I. Pl. 6.12. On three pieces of butts a curved channel can be seen, as in I. Pl. 6.17. No doubt it is meant for a line which would secure the foreshaft in case of a fracture. L3:13602, from layer 3, is a fragment of the butt of a foreshaft made of walrus penis bone, and carefully trimmed. Immediately above the scarf there is also a curved channel, placed a little obliquely.

Cylindrical socket-pieces for harpoons. — Three fragments resembling that shown in I. Pl. 6.9. Two are of narwhal tusk, one of bone; their lengths are 3—4 cm. — A socket-piece of similar shape, but only 1.5 × 1.3 cm, and made of narwhal tusk, is most likely from a child's harpoon. All are from layers 2 and 3.

Finger rests. — Two specimens from layers 1 and 4, of the type with one hole, like that in I. Pl. 5.28 were found.

Harpoon rest (?) of baleen. — L3:14426 and 14519, both from layer 7, resemble that shown in I. Pl. 45.17. They may be harpoon rests used at breathing-hole hunting.

Lance heads. — L3:14689, from layer 8, is a movable lance head of bone, of a pointed-oval cross-section, 2.9 × 1.3—1.7 cm. The length is now 25 cm, but the fore end is broken. The butt is conical with a rounded end, and five centimeters from the end is a transverse hole. L3:13768, from layer 4, is a fragmentary middle part of a lance head of similar cross-section. L3:14492—14493, from layer 7, together form one piece of a lance head, 3.2 cm broad, with a large, open blade slit and plug hole. In layer 6 a small fragment of a similar lance head was found.

L3:13551, from 3, layer and L3:13900, from layer 5, are broken fore-ends of more slender lance heads; breadth 1.7 cm. The latter has two small, longitudinally placed holes connected by a lashing groove for the blade.

Lance blade. — L3:13475, from layer 3, is a fragment of a large slate lance blade, 6.2 cm broad, broken at a central hole.

Ice picks. — Six specimens from layers 7—8 were found, three of them of antler, and three of bone. The butts have a scarf, and two specimens have a transverse hole, like that in I. Pl. 7.8. Two complete ice picks are 11.5 and 12.5 cm long, and a crudely made specimen of whale bone is 19 cm long. — Eleven pieces, from layers 2—7, are most likely fragments of ice picks.

Wound pins. — Two almost complete wound pins of antler resemble that shown in I. Pl. 9.3. They are 10 cm long. Of four fragments three are of antler. L3:14290 is of walrus ivory; in the blade part there are two longitudinal grooves.

Sealing stool leg. — Four specimens from layers 4.5 and 7, of length 10—11.5 cm. They taper towards both ends, like that in I. Pl. 8.5. Three of them are of wood. L3:14291, from layer 7, is of bone.

Side prongs for bird dart. — L3:14631, from layer 7, length 13 cm, has two inside barbs, like that in I. Pl. 10.8. The end of the butt has, on the inner side, a rather sharp edge, which a little towards the front is flattened into a plane rest. L3:14368, also from layer 7, is of similar shape, except that the butt is broken off. On L3:14369 the butt has a broad and plane inner side. The fore-end has been broken, but the remaining piece has been re-fashioned into an eight centimeter long bodkin with a slender point, the preserved part of which is two centimeters long. All the three specimens mentioned are of antler. — L3:13635, from layer 4, is a broken butt with a flat step on the inner side, almost like that shown in I. Pl. 10.7.

Throwing boards. — L3:13521, from layer 3, is a fragment of the front end of a throwing board. The end is flattened, and it is split at the slanting hole for the bone tenon. L3:14182, from layer 6, is a fragment of a rear end, with a powerfully fashioned handle.

Of round, *wooden weapon shafts* twelve fragments were found, some of them with a scarf.

Bows. — L3:14494, from layer 7, is a small fragment of a wooden bow. L3:13429, from layer 2, is a broken end of a piece of a bow of antler. — Three ends of *baleen bows* were found in layers 3, 7 and 8. The ends of two children's bows of baleen were found in layers 5 and 7.

Bow braces. — L3:14690, from layer 8, is a flat bow brace of antler. Its middle part is slightly sunken, as in I. fig. 106.20, to form a bed for the sinew backing. L3:14292, from layer 7, which resembles it, is 10.5 cm long and 2.4 cm broad. Together with the latter was found a brace of antler for the inner side of a bow, (L3:14325), resembling that in I. Pl. 10.23. L3:13848, from layer 5, resembles the last mentioned specimen, but is of bone and rather heavy, 1.2 cm thick in the middle. The flattened ends are slightly concave on the bow side. Its breadth is 2.1 cm, and the length can be seen to have been about 12.5 cm.

Arrow heads. — L3:14666, from layer 8, is of antler, slender and round, with a *short, unsymmetrical blade part*, like that in I. Pl. 11.8. The ends are broken. — Three almost complete arrow heads of antler have a *lanceolate blade part*, like that in I. Pl. 11.10. Of these L3:14179, from layer 6, can be seen to have had two knobs on the tang. On L3:13701, which is 13.5 cm long, the tang has one knob on one side, two on the other. L3:14524, from layer 7, has the tang sharply set off from the shank. In addition, two fragments of blades were found. Two small arrow heads of similar type, 7 and 8 cm long, one of them made of bone, belonged to children's arrows.

L3:13832, from layer 5, is a small, round arrow head 7.8 cm long, of antler, with a short, widened blade part which on one side ends in *a barb*. L3:14293, from layer 7, and 12.5 cm long, has a short, unilateral blade part about 3.5 cm long and 1.9 cm broad, of which the rear is almost at right angles to the shank. The tang has two knobs at unequal heights. In addition, two broken tangs with knobs were found.

Two fore-ends, 19 butts, and four other fragments of wooden *arrow shafts* were found in the layers 3—8.

Salmon spears. — Four pointed bone sticks with their rear ends flattened are most likely the *center prongs* of three-pronged salmon spears. Their lengths are 8—13.5 cm.

Barbs for salmon spears. — Two antler sticks with an oval cross-section, having a rounded point and a scarf, almost like that in I. Pl. 13.11. Of these L3:14085, from layer 6, is 7 cm long; L3:14726, from layer 8, is 6 cm long. On L3:14585, from layer 7, shown on Pl. 3.9, the end of the scarf has a small groove as if for a cord, which may be a later addition. — In Pt. I, p. 218 I have described such points as barbs for salmon spears, as this seems to be the most obvious explanation. To judge from the shape, however, some of them might also be points for two-pronged bird arrows, which are known from West Greenland among other places[1]).

L3:13305, from layer 2, shown on Pl. 4.7, resembles a finger rest with three lashing holes (cf. I. Pl. 5.25). It is, however, only 0.8 cm thick, and is pointed, with a sharp convexe edge next to the point, the point itself being slightly rounded, presumably by wear. It is 6.3 cm long and 2.4 cm broad. It may be a barb for a salmon spear. — Some doubt may also arise about the use of L3:13524, from layer 3. It is made of antler, is 5.3 cm long, and has, on the inner side a step, and at one extremity an obliquely cut lashing groove, thus resembling in shape the object from Nûgdlît shown in fig. 61.

---

[1]) K. Birket-Smith: Ethnography of the Egedesminde District, 1924, p. 344.

L3:13479, from layer 3, is a crudely made *leister prong* of bone with a heavy inside barb and a notch on the outer side, roughly in the middle. — L3:14028, Pl. 3.11, is presumably a leister prong of baleen.

Leister harpoon heads. — L3:13580, from layer 3, is a 6.8 cm long, slender head of antler with many small, opposite barbs placed close

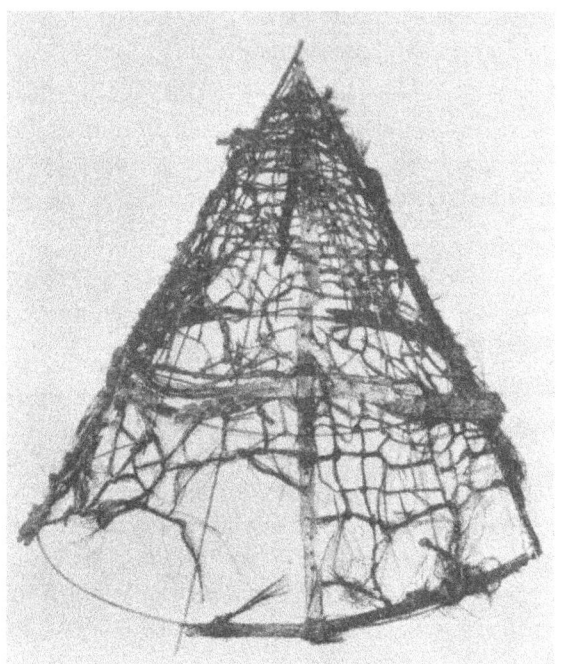

Fig. 63. Catcher of baleen, from Comer's midden, Thule.

to one another, in type resembling that shown in I. Pl. 1.8. L3:13933, from layer 6, is the end part of a similar head of walrus ivory.

L3:13675, from layer 4, is a 10 cm long, slender *trout needle* of antler, resembling that in I. Pl. 14.6.

Baleen catcher. — L3:14459, from layer 7, fig. 63, is the larger part of a baleen catcher. The frame-work consists of two 1—1.4 cm broad strips which cross one another at the bottom, and which are tied to two concentric rings, one of which is 15 cms above the other. Of the upper ring, which forms the rim of the catcher, only little is left. The netting of baleen cord is tied to the strips, which, with the exception of the one forming the rim, are perforated at intervals of one centimeter. The netting consists of vertical and horizontal cords, tied together with clove-hitches, simple knots, or more or less loose turns. The depth of the catcher was about 42 cm, and the diameter of the rim about the same. It is most likely a bird catcher used for hunting little auks.

Gull hooks. — Five specimens were found in layers 2, 6 and 7. All are of the common type: wooden with an oblique groove, like that shown in I. Pl. 14.7. All are more or less damaged.

L3:14692, from layer 8, is a *bone gorge*, 12 cm long. The line hole is placed four centimeters from one end. The breadth of the gorge at the hole is 0.7 cm, decreasing towards the pointed ends. In the hole a piece of baleen line is still preserved.

Fish hook. — L3:13941, from layer 6, (Pl. 3.8), is a fish hook, 8.2 cm long, made from a piece of antler. The long branch is flattened into a wedge-shape and provided with a hole and a notch in the end where the line had been attached. The short branch has a separate inset point of walrus ivory.

Bola weight. — A bola weight of bone, (L3:14296), was found in layer 7. It is roughly wedge-shaped and has an obliquely placed, transverse hole. Its length is 6.5 cm.

Toggles. — L3:13538, from layer 3, (Pl. 4.9), is a small, shuttle-shaped toggle made of narwhal tusk, 3.5 cm long and 0.7 cm broad, with a notch in the middle of one side. — L3:13687, from layer 4, (Pl. 4.10), is a toggle of walrus ivory, 5.3 cm long, with a double curve and a central, funnel-shaped hole, which is widest at the convex side. Although it seems rather heavy for the purpose, it may be a toggle-shaped thimble holder. — Two other small toggles with an oblong hole, L3:14078 of antler and L3:14297 of bone, from layers 6 and 7, resemble that shown in I. Pl. 16.8.

Ferrules. — L3:13735 from layer 4, and L3:13871 from layer 5, are two flat ferrules made of antler, of a similar shape to those shown in I. Pl. 9.13-14, but with the rear end cut off straight. They are 2 and 2.2 cm broad respectively, their lengths being 3.8 and 2.4 cm, and their thickness 1 and 0.7 cm. Both have a hole for a peg, and in L3:13871 remnants of wood can be seen. They seem to be too tiny for kayak paddles; nevertheless the possibility that at least the latter has been used as an end mounting for a pointed kayak paddle cannot be disregarded. Another possibility is that they may have belonged to snow beaters (cf. I, p. 221).

Bone "bolt". — L3:13710, from layer 4, is a fragment of a heavy bone "bolt", or nail, with a head, and of a rectangular cross-section, 1.1 × 0.9 cm, resembling that in I. Pl. 9.23. The end is broken. L3:13847, from layer 5, is a broken point of a similar nail. The end is a four-sided pyramid-shape. — From the find of an umiaq in Peary Land by Eigil

Knuth it now appears that such large bone nails had been used for jointing the heavy timber of umiaqs[1]).

Wooden pegs. — Fourteen wooden pegs used for sledge shoes were found, most of them, like that shown in I. Pl. 12.28, with an obliquely cut off rear end. They are from the layers 4—7.

Sledge. — A piece of wood about 10 cm long was found in layer 1. It has many lashing holes, and most probably comes from a *compound sledge runner*, (cf. I. Pl. 15.11).

A total of 75 fragments of *sledge shoes* were found, 58 of them of bone, 17 of ivory. Fifteen of those of bone and ten of those of ivory have lashing holes, placed in pairs, as on those shown in I. Pl. 15.6-7. Four specimens have both peg holes and lashing holes, the rest only peg holes. The latter is true of all sledge shoes of bone from layers 6—8, where the manner of fastening could be ascertained.

Four broken ends of the *cross-slats* of sledges, from layers 6—7, are of whale bone. They each have one pair of opposite lashing notches, and on three of the specimens a groove leads to the end on the upper side, as shown in I. Pl. 15.10. L3:14699, from layer 8, is a wooden cross-slat for a small child's sledge. It is 16.2 cm long and 3.2 cm broad, tapering a little towards the ends, which have two pairs of opposite notches and a groove, as above.

Trace buckles. — A total of thirteen trace buckles were found, resembling those shown in I. Pl. 16.27, 28, 30. Two of them are unfinished, and on one, made of antler, the two holes merge into one larger one. Eight are of walrus ivory, four of bone. They come from all the layers 1—8. — Two trace buckles, from layers 6—7, are of baleen, like that in I. Pl. 46.13, one of them, however, being more elongated.

Ferrule for a whip shank. — L3:13257, from layer 1, Pl. 4.4, is a ferrule of bone for a small whip shank; such ferrules being called "kange" by the Polar eskimos. It is flat, with an oblong hole for the end of the shank, and has a hook-shaped extension on one side. Its size is $3 \times 1.2 \times 0.9$ cm.

Baleen stick. — Four broad, broken butts of heavy baleen sticks come from the layers 7—8. Three of them have a hole for a strap, as in I. Pl. 46.10-11. L3:14454 has two opposite notches instead of a hole. Several such sticks have been found before (see I. p. 274), but their purpose is not knowvn. They may have been used as dog sticks used when feeding the dogs.

Umiaq ribs. — Two fragments of wooden umiaq ribs, each with a concave end, as shown in I. Pl. 17.2, are from layers 7—8.

---

[1]) E. Knuth: Et umiak-fund i Peary Land. — Fra Nationalmuseets Arbejdsmark. 1951; pp. 77—87. København 1951.

Harpoon rest for a kayak. — L3:13705, from layer 4, is a wooden harpoon rest 10 cm long and 5 cm high, of a type resembling that in I. Pl. 18.14. In the middle is an oval, transverse hole for a wooden stick, and next to this is a rectangular hollow. Near the edge itself there is a small hole with lashing grooves on both sides. L3:13830, from layer 5, is of bone and in shape resembles that shown in I. Pl. 18.21.

Leg of a kayak rack. — L3:14694, from layer 8, shown on Pl. 4.13, is most likely such a leg. It is 14.2 m long, made of a flat piece of antler. It is a little curved, and on the convex side, where it is broadest, it has a rest, two centimeters high, with a transverse hole at each end, so that it fits the bottom, or frame of the rack. The upper three centimeters taper to a rounded end.

Snow knives. — Six snow knives of bone were found in the layers 5—8. They are of a type similar to those in I. Pl. 18.3-4, having a distinct kink where the back meets the handle. Only L3:14695, from layer 8, differs in having a knob with a hole for a strap at the bend, which is not so pronounced as on the other specimens. In addition to these, twenty fragments were found, mainly of blades of similar bone snow knives.

Snow probes. — L3:13849, from layer 5, is a 15 cm long fragment of a snow probe of bone with an egg-shaped extension of the fore end, like that in I. Pl. 17.19. The end is a little flattened on one side. L3:14322, from layer 7, is presumably a fragment of a similar snow probe.

Bone knife. — L3:13423, from layer 2, is a fragment of an antler blade, 9 cm long and 2.6 cm broad, with blunt edges on both sides (cf. I. Pl. 19.1-2). The fore-end is broken, but two lashing holes indicate that it had been repaired. The handle is also broken, but at the transition to the blade it has two narrow, parallel, ornamental rolls on the outer side of the antler.

Baleen knife. — L3:14281, from layer 6, is a one-edged baleen knife (cf. I. Pl. 49.6, 13). The transition from the blade to the broader, straight handle is marked by two shoulders. The end of the blade is broken, but the total length can be judged to have been about 22 cm.

Knives with end blades. — A total of eleven complete handles, and three split-off fragments of fore-ends were found in the layers 4—8. L3:13637, from layer 4, made of antler, is straight, 10.3 cm long, the fore-end being a little broader than the butt where it has a strap hole. Around the blade end there is a lashing groove. L3:14527, from layer 7, is 11.5 cm long and slightly curved, made of the root end of an antler, the small, knobbed collar of which forms a convenient support for the hand. L3:14568, also from layer 7, is shown on Pl. 3.1. It is 14 cm long, made of antler. The thicker, middle part, of the handle forms a wide belt, which, on all sides, is ornamented with longitudinal grooves. On the concave, narrow side, at both ends, these grooves are crossed by transverse grooves. In the butt there is a transverse hole, and, leading into this, there is also a hole drilled from the end. — L3:14074, from layer 6, is 11 cm long, made of antler, having a strap hole, and, on one side, four knobs, resembling those seen in I. Pl. 19.19. L3:13919, from layer 5, is 10.5 cm long, made of antler. At the butt end it has a unilateral knob and a strap hole, like that in I. Pl. 19.24.

L3:14670, from layer 8, is part of a knife handle with a unilateral end knob and ornamented in a "herring-bone" pattern. The fore-end has a scarf. — L3:14240, from layer 6, is a heavier bone knife handle 15.5 cm long, with a very long unilateral end knob which has a hole drilled in the direction of the handle. L3:13836, from layer 5, is 14 cm long, made of bone, broadest at the butt where it has a hole.

L3:14375, from layer 7, and L3:14719, from layer 8, are simple *whittling knives* of antler, 8 and 11 cm long. L3:14569, from layer 7, is of bone, 13.5 cm long, rectangular in cross-section, almost like that in I. Pl. 20.5. The blade socket is only 0.8 cm long, and the fore-end has, on each side, a wide, rounded groove leading to the end. 2.5 cm from the fore-end there is a transverse hole. L3:13736, from layer 4, is like the latter, but is only 7.8 cm long, with a 0.6 cm long blade socket.

Knife handle made from two halves (splitting knife). — L3:13837, from layer 5, is part of such a handle, and resembles that in I. Pl. 21.7. It is 7 cm long, and is made of bone.

Flensing knife. — L3:13944, from layer 6, is a knife handle with an open blade slit in the fore-end. In this end there is also a peg hole for securing the blade. The handle is 11.2 cm long, crudely made from a piece of antler which has been cut off straight.

Knife with side blade. — L3:15759, from layer 4, is a fragment of a simple antler knife with a groove for a side blade. Almost as in I. Pl. 20.26 the blade part merges evenly into the handle which is provided with a strap hole. L3:14215, from layer 6, and L3:13610, from layer 3, are broken ends of antler blade parts. L3:13609, also from layer 3, is the butt of an antler blade part. It tapers a little, and is fashioned as if to be inserted into a separate handle, (cf. I. Pl. 20.31).

On L3:13611, from layer 3, the remains of *two grooves for side blades* can be seen on one side. It is crudely made of bone, the flat handle passing evenly into the blade part.

Three knives have grooves for an *end blade and side blade on one side*. L3:14038, from layer 6, is of bone, 21 cm long. The handle passes evenly into the somewhat flattened blade part, which at the fore-end has a hole for a peg or a lashing. The handle has four finger notches on one side and a strap hole in the butt. L3:13465, from layer 3, is a 12 cm long blade part of a similar knife. The fore-end is broken at a peg hole. L3:14671, from layer 8, is also a blade part made of antler. The butt has a scarf and a peg hole, to fit a separate handle. L3:13483, from layer 3, is a blade part made of narwhal tusk, 12 cm long. It has a groove, and a peg hole for an end blade. A blade groove 2.7 cm long can be seen in the middle of one side and two longer grooves on the other side.

L3:13579, from layer 4, is a small antler knife with a *slender handle and broad blade part*, as in I. Pl. 21.15. The handle is broken. The blade part is 3.5 × 1.7 cm, and in the blade groove there is a remnant of an iron blade.

Twelve fragments of knife handles could not be identified as to type.

Knife blades of slate. — L3:13638, from layer 4, is the point of a rather heavy and crudely made two-edged blade of slate, 5 cm broad. L3:14564, from layer 7, is a broken piece of a 0.25 cm thick and 3.5 cm broad two-edged blade, with two holes.

L3:14572, from layer 7, is a split-off piece of silicious slate, 7.5 × 4.5 cm, with the sharp, convex edge ground. Most likely it had been used as a knife, without any separate handle.

Ulos. — Three ulo handles, of which two are split-off halves, all from layers 6—7, are of the low, thick type shown in I. Pl. 22.9, 11. Two of them are 8 cm long, and made of bone; one specimen, only 5 cm long, is made of narwhal tusk. L3:14258, which is made of bone, has the end slanting to form a more convenient rest for the index finger. L3:13511, from layer 3, is of a similar shape, but with the sides converging towards the blade edge, thus forming an acute angle.

L3:13737, from layer 4, which is made of antler, is flat, 4.5 cm long and 2.5 cm high. In the middle, next to the back, is a small oblong hole. L3:14645, from layer 7, is also quite flat, made from a piece of a whale epiphysis. It is irregularly trapezoidal, almost like that in I. Pl. 22.15. It is 9 cm broad, almost 6 cm high, and in the 4 cm long lower edge there is a blade groove only 2 cm long.

L3:14503, from layer 7, is trapezoidal with a rounded thicker back, resembling that in I. Pl. 22.20, except that it has an oblong hollow for the finger on each side. L3:13870, from layer 5, is flat, trapezoidal, with a large, approximately trapezoidal opening.

L3:13318, from layer 2, is the blade part of a *compound ulo*, resembling that in I. Pl. 23.5, but with only one central hole at the upper edge. Another hole has been drilled at one side, nearer to the lower edge. The upper edge has been thinned down for insertion into a groove in the handle.

An ulo with an iron blade of *modern type* was found in the top layer. The blade is a pointed-oval, and the stem is made from a brass tube, hammered flat.

Hand drill. — One specimen, L3:14376, from layer 7, has a tapering handle of wood 6.5 cm long, and a thin iron point 1.2 cm long. Also the implement shown on Pl. 3.7, L3:14086, from layer 6, is most likely a hand drill.

Bow drills. — L3:13558, from layer 3, is a *bow drill shank* of antler, 10.2 cm long, resembling that shown in I. Pl. 24.11. L3:14377, from layer 7, is 14 cm long, more slender, with the middle part narrowed in a little. Four drill shanks are made of wood, and are 9.5—21 cm long. L3:13417, the largest of them, has an iron bit, presumably made from a thick nail, the point of which has been filed thin. — Two butts of drill shanks have their fore-ends made into a scarf, one of them with a step like that in I. Pl. 24.13.

L3:13375, from layer 2, may be the fore-end of a drill shank of bone, broken but re-fashioned, with a 2.5 cm long, flat tang for insertion in a wooden shank. The total length is 9 cm. At the fore-end there is a raised roll. The socket in the fore-end is a little irregular, about 0.5 cm in diameter.

A *drill mouth piece* of caribou astragalus, like that in I. Pl. 24.25, was found in layer 7.

Baleen saw. — L3:14660, from layer 7, is 22.5 cm long, somewhat like that in I. Pl. 49.13 in shape, except that the handle is broader and the blade has evenly curved edges. One edge has remnants of small, almost worn off teeth placed close together. L3:14452, also from layer 7, is a broken blade part, 19 cm long and 2.3 cm broad at the handle end, the breadth gradually decreasing towards the pointed fore end. It has small saw teeth on one edge. — L3:13755, from layer 4, is a 19 cm long and 1.7 cm broad strip of baleen, decreasing in breadth towards one end, where crude teeth have been cut on one side along a length of six centimeters.

Stone scraper. — A total of 57 blunt scrapers, or rubbing stones of dolomite, like those shown in I. Pl. 25.16, 19, were found. They come from all the layers 1—7. Nine stones without discernible fashioning may also have been used as rubbing stones.

Seven scrapers, from layers 2—8, made of a slate-like stone, have a crudely fashioned scraping edge which has become rounded by wear. On L3:14380, from layer 7, which is 8.5 cm long, a thicker part of the stone forms a handle, the thinner part forming a flat blade 1.5 cm broad with a rounded end.

Scraper of bone. — Nine narrow scrapers made of more or less crudely worked pieces of bone, two of narwhal tusk, and one, L3:13353, from a seal's radius. The breadth of the fore-ends varies from 5.5 cm to just a rounded point, (cf. I. Pl. 26.17, 18). — L3:13971, from layer 6, seen on Pl. 3.3, is a scraper of subtriangular shape, 8 × 6 cm, made from a flat piece of a polar bear mandible, resembling that in I. Pl. 26.9, but of a more regular shape.

L3:13287, from the top layer, is a modern scraper with a curved iron blade and a wooden handle, of the type shown in Steensby: Ethnology and Anthropogeography of the Polar Eskimos, fig. 27, p. 336.

Two-handed scraper. — L3:14529, from layer 7, Pl. 3.5, is a two-handed scraper 18 cm long, made from a piece of *antler* cut through longitudinally. One end is the natural end of the antler, the other has been made into a point. L3:14192, from layer 6, is a fragment of a two-handed scraper made from a *bear's ulna*.

Whetstones. — A total of 47 whetstones were found throughout all the layers.

Hammer stone. — Three specimens, in shape almost like that in I. Pl. 29.27 were found.

Adze heads. — L3:14300, Pl. 3.2, from layer 7, is an adze head of bone, 10 cm long. On the under side is a faintly hollowed bed for the shaft, and on the other three sides a broad, deeply sunken area for the lashing. L3:14756, from layer 8, is also of bone, 11.5 cm long and 5 cm broad. It has a deeper hollow on the under side, and three pairs of *vertical holes*, almost like that shown in I. Pl. 28.11. Anteriorly, there are two more vertical holes, which on the upper side are connected by a groove, each hole having been made by drilling two holes close together and removing the intermediate wall. L3:14697, also from layer 8, is of antler. It has a flat bed for the handle, three *horizontal holes*, and a curved hole more to the front of the under side, like that in I. Pl. 28.15.

Bone wedges. — Eight specimens were found.

Marline spikes. — Two specimens, L3:13707 from layer 4 and L3:14243 from layer 6, crudely made of bone, with flat, rounded points, and in shape resembling that in I.Pl. 29.15. L3:14302, from layer 7, is a flat marline spike of narwhal tusk. L3:13532, from layer 3, and 13425, from layer 2, are made from small branches of antler with the ends flattened. The latter has part of an adjoining branch attached to it, so as to form a handle. L3:13926, from layer 5, is made from a flat piece of antler, one end of which has been narrowed into a slender point which is now broken. The butt has a unilateral end knob. — L3:14125 and 14465 are pointed marline spikes, 10.5 and 9.5 cm long, made of bone and antler respectively. — L3:13512, from layer 3, and L3:13999, from layer 6, are pieces of antler 7.5 and 10.5 cm long with narrow, sharp-edged points. L3:13920 is of bone, 8 cm long, almost like that in I. Pl. 29.17, but having only one hole.

An implement made from a *fibula*, (L3:13776, from layer 4), is 9.5 cm long and has a strong, sharp-edged point. L3:14720, from layer 8, is a pointed seal fibula, and L3:14636, from layer 7, a pointed *caribou ulna*, like that in I. Pl. 29.2.

Bodkins. — Two small, pointed pieces, one of antler, the other of bone, may have been used as bodkins. L3:13401, from layer 2, is an 18 cm long bodkin made from a small ulna. L3:13934, from layer 6, is made from a pointed bird beak, 8.5 cm long, resembling that shown in I. Pl. 36.4.

L3:13952, from layer 6, shown on Pl. 4.11, is a heavy, round bodkin of walrus ivory, 9.5 cm long. It has two ornamental rolls, the outer one forming, at its end, a head with a small hole drilled from one side diagonally towards the end.

Mattocks. — Two broken rear ends of whale bone mattock heads both from layer 6, having a bed for the handle and a row of deep notches at the sides, almost as in I. Pl. 30.21.

Cutting board. — L3:14379, from layer 7, and L3:14722, from layer 8, are two flat pieces of whale bone, about 15 × 10 cm, with marks made by cutting or hewing on one side.

L3:14451, from layer 7, shown on Pl. 3.12, is presumably a *baleen cutting board*, of a peculiar "human-like" shape. It seems, however, that it had not been used as no cutting marks can be seen.

Eight pieces of *pyrites* were found in the layers 2—7, and in layer 8 a piece of wood, (L3:14675), with two deep hollows from *fire drilling* was also found.

Lamps. — L3:13683, from layer 4, is a corner of a small soapstone lamp with remnants of a *ledge* at a distance of two centimeters from the front edge. L3:14194, from layer 6, is a fragment of a thin-walled lamp, also with a ledge. — A fragment of a larger lamp, L3:13712, from layer 4, has a *step* two centimeters from the front edge, like that shown in I. Pl. 32.9. L3:13872, from layer 5, is a small fragment of a similar lamp. — A small, shallow lamp of the modern crescent shape, 15 × 9.5 cm, with a line etched along the front edge, comes from layer 1. — In addition, four unidentifiable fragments of soapstone lamps were found.

Lamp trimmers. — L3:13535, from layer 3, is a slender stick of *asbestos*, 11 cm long. L3:13359, from layer 2, is a fragment, apparently of a similar lamp trimmer.

Seven specimens are made from simple willow twigs, and 55 are various wooden sticks. Of the latter L3:14195, from layer 6, Pl. 3.4, is peculiar in having a bird's beak lashed to the rear end with baleen cord. — Two lamp trimmers from layers 1 and 2 have the rear end fashioned to fit a "swallow tail" notch in a separate handle, (cf. I. Pl. 31.22), and L3:13780, from layer 4, has a scarf and a lashing groove.

Cooking pots. — A total of fifty fragments of soapstone pots were found, but none of them large enough to allow a safe determination of their shape. One fragment from layer 4, L3:13713, had been repaired with a flat strip of iron.

A small piece of worked soapstone, L3:13421, from layer 2, can be seen to be a fragment of the side of a shallow *soapstone bowl* only 2.5 cm high with traces of meat left on the inside.

Meat trays. — Twenty-eight fragments of hollow wooden meat trays were found.

Oval bowls. — L3:14546, from layer 7, is the wooden bottom of an oval bowl, 10 × 6.2 cm. In addition, five fragments of similar bottoms were found, in the layers 3, 6 and 7. — L3:14200, from layer 6, is the greater part of a small, oval wooden cup bottom, 6.7 × 4 cm.

L3:14362 is a fragment of a *baleen handle*, wound round with baleen cord.

Tub stave. — Four wooden tub staves were found in the layers 4, 6, 7 and 8. Two specimens, L3:13597, from layer 3, and L3:14317, from layer 7, may also be tub staves, and so may a badly weathered specimen, L3:13599, from layer 3, which is of oak and has a hole at one end. L3:13577, also from layer 3, is a piece 4.5 cm broad, which, no doubt, formed the top part of a tub stave. In the lower edge it has a groove, and it had been made secure by four small pegs.

Wooden box. — L3:14251, from layer 6, is a rectangular side of a four-sided wooden box. The specimen is 12.5 × 7 cm. It has holes for pegs along three edges, the pegs being partly preserved. At a distance of 1.5 cm from the upper edge and 0.7 cm from the middle, a small, slightly slanting bone peg had been inserted, and below this peg there is a faint hollow in the wood with a peg hole at each side, one with remnants of a wooden peg. No doubt this formed part of a lock.

Mountings for skin vessels. — A slender wooden stick, L3:13821, from layer 5, 11.5 cm long, with both ends pointed as shown in I. Pl. 35.24, is most likely a *rib* for a skin vessel. L3:13851, also from layer 5, is 10.5 cm long and 1.7 cm broad and has its ends flattened. L3:14043, from layer 6, seems to be a similar rib. It is now 19.5 cm long, but one end is broken.

Four fragments of bone strips about 1.5 cm broad with two shallow longitudinal grooves on one side, as shown in I. Pl. 35.8, and having a row of holes close together, as in I. Pl. 35.5, are most likely pieces of *bone rims*. They were found in the layers 2, 3 and 4.

Edge mounting. — Three fragments of mountings of antler, 0.4—0.6 cm broad, from layers 3—4, resemble that shown in I. Pl. 35.7. Three flatter pieces, which were found in the layers 6 and 7, are about 1 cm broad, resembling that in I. Pl. 35.4, two of them having a concave under side. — Four more fragments of flat bone mountings were found, the use of which cannot be ascertained.

Carrying handle. — A broken end of a rather crudely made, slightly curved bone stick, (L3:13336, from layer 2), may be a fragment of a carrying handle. It is about 0.8 × 0.8 cm in cross-section and has a wide notch at the end of the convex side. — L3:14553, from layer 7, is presumably a wooden handle for a bowl or the like. It is slightly curved, and of a nearly oval cross-section, 0.9 × 0.5 cm in the middle, decreasing towards the ends, which are made into small tenons. Its length is 9.4 cm.

L3:14428, from layer 7, is the end of a 1.5 cm broad baleen strip, which at its end has two oblong notches, like that in I. Pl. 48.16.

L3:13747, from layer 4, seems to be a fragment of the handle of a *wooden ladle* of a shape similar to that in I. Pl. 34.6.

Sucking tube. — L3:14739, from layer 8, is a 10 cm long fragment of a sucking tube of narwhal tusk. It ends in a roll, as shown in I. Pl. 34.16. Its width is 1.5 cm.

Meat sticks. — L3:14528, from layer 7, is a meat stick, 16 cm long, made from a curved, pointed ulna. L3:13291, from layer 1, is 21 cm long and is carefully made from a rib.

Platform mat of baleen. — Seven fragments of baleen mats were found, like that shown in I. fig. 96. They come from the layers 3—7.

Snow beater. — L3:13492, from layer 3, is, most likely, a broken end, 12.5 cm long, of a heavy bone snow beater. Its cross-section is a flat oval, and at the fracture its breadth is 4.3 cm, gradually decreasing towards the rounded end, (cf. I. Pl. 31.2). L3:13704, from layer 4, is possibly the butt of a similar bone snow beater. It is narrowed a little to form a handle, and ends in a large, bilateral knob.

A total of 45 more or less fragmentary specimens of *baleen snow beaters* were found. Of these eight are fore-ends. The shape of the butt varies considerably. Fourteen specimens have a unilateral end knob, like that on I. Pl. 45.2, 3. In addition L3:14280 has a row of smaller knobs on one side of the handle. Fourteen other specimens have bilateral, symmetrically extended butts as in I. Pl. 45.11, two of these having in addition, one a round and the other a triangular hole. On L3:14356, from layer 7, the butt has the shape of an obtuse angle, as in I. Pl. 46.3.' On L3:14029, from layer 6, the end is concave, as in I. Pl. 46.7, and has a triangular hole. L3:14453, from layer 7, fig. 64, has two small, bipartite knobs and three holes, of which two are circular and a larger one is oval. On L3:13826, from layer 5, L3:14061 and 14276, from layer 6, the butt is unsymmetrical, almost as in I. Pl.

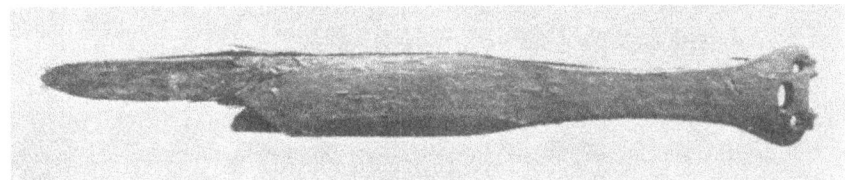

Fig. 64. Baleen snow beater. Comer's midden, Thule.

45.8-10. A single specimen, L3:14279, has an evenly tapering handle with a row of small notches on each side, and on L3:14627 the rounded butt has two notches opposite one another, most likely for a strap.

Comb. — L3:14548, from layer 7, is a broken tooth of a walrus ivory comb. A small hole at the fracture shows that it had once been repaired. — L3:14761, Pl. 3.10, is a *baleen* comb with only three coarse teeth.

A small, disk-like *bead of soapstone*, L3:14587, from layer 7, which resembles that in I. Pl. 37.21 was found. Its diameter is 0.65 cm. — L3:13953, from layer 6, shown on Pl. 4.5, is obviously a link of a *chain ornament* of walrus ivory. The central, four-sided and thicker part has a hole drilled longitudinally through it, and the flat "wings" each have a transverse hole. The whole is 1.1 cm long, 1.7 cm broad, and 0.8 cm thick.

Only one *bear's tooth* with a suspension hole was found, in layer 6. — A *tooth pendant*, L3:14506, from layer 7, from a fox canine, like that shown in I. Pl. 38.23 was also found. L3:13460, from layer 2, is a small walrus molar with a hole drilled through the root. The same is true of L3:13459, also a walrus molar, 4 cm long, which, however, has the sides roughly fashioned by hewing.

A *pendant*, L3:13688, from layer 4, made of a green stone, has the shape of a truncated cone with a roll-like extension and a hole drilled through longitudinally. It is 1 cm long and 1.2 cm in diameter.

Drum. — A small fragment of a *bone drum frame*, L3:14252, from layer 6, 2.2 cm broad. On the outer side it has a deep groove, and the upper edge is made thin, as shown in I. fig. 102.3. — A *drum handle*, L3:13380, from layer 2, which is 6 cm long, is made of the drilled off root of a rudimentary narwhal tusk. It has a deep, transverse groove, also made by drilling, and two lashing holes, one on each side of the groove.

Amulet box. — An amulet box of wood, L3:14390, found in layer 7, is almost 9 cm long and 2 cm broad, with one compartment. A flat *lid* for an amulet box, L3:14010, from layer 6, is 3.4×1.7 cm; the two longer edges are a little concave.

Ajagaq. — A broken off end of a large *seal radius*, L3:13789, from layer 4, has six holes drilled in its end, the holes being placed so as to form a triangle. Four of the holes pass obliquely right through the sides of the bone. L3:13443, from layer 2, is a fragment of a similar joint, but having only one wide hole. — L3:14442, from layer 7, is most likely also an ajagaq, made from a heavy *seal humerus* of which a part has been hewn off. The end where the hole should be is damaged, but in the middle of the bone there is a roughened belt where the string had apparently been tied on.

Forty seven *gambling bones* from seal phalanges, like those in I. Pl. 39.23, were found in the layers 2—7.

Of carved *animal figures* a crudely made wooden bear figure was found in layer 4, and a small dog figure of walrus ivory in layer 1.

Dolls. — Eleven wooden dolls, most of them damaged, were found. They are of the type with flat faces and no arms, or arms only indicated, like those in I. Pl. 40.2-3. One specimen, L3:14051, from layer 6, represents a woman with a toupee, like that shown in I. Pl. 40.15. On two specimens, also from layer 6, the tops of the boots are indicated. One of these, L3:14144, also a female, has exaggerated broad hips and a small bust.

L3:14507, from layer 7, is a fragment of a small doll of walrus ivory. A similar one was found in layer 1. L3:13787, from layer 4, is a female doll made of narwhal tusk, 7.5 cm high, and with very broad shoulders. The head is now missing, but two small lashing holes indicate that it had once been tied on after having been broken.

A slender doll, L3:13877, found in layer 5, 9.5 cm long, is crudely made of baleen.

Top pivots. — One specimen, L3:14044, from layer 6, is 10 cm long, and resembles that in I. Pl. 42.7. Two other wooden specimens, from layer 7, are 10.5 and 12 cm long, the latter having the lower end more extended, like that in I. Pl. 42.6.

A *toy bow*, L3:13301, found in layer 1, is made of a flat strip of bone, 1.1 cm broad, cut from a rib. The middle part is a little thicker and broader than the rest. One end is broken, but the total length can be seen to have been about 30 cm. — Six butts from *toy arrows* were found, in addition to a lanceolate *toy arrow head* of baleen, (L3:13729), which is 10 cm long.

The handle part of a wooden *toy sling handle*, L3:14254, was found in layer 6, and a fragment of a similar handle, L3:14509, in layer 7. In shape they resemble that in I. Pl. 42.27.

A *toy sealing stool seat* of wood, found in layer 7, is shown on Pl. 3.6. It is 4.3 × 2 cm. On the under side, near the middle of the straight edge, there is an oblong hollow, presumably representing a handle.

L3:14050, from layer 6, is the pointed fore-end of a *toy wooden sledge runner*. In the upper edge small notches have been cut for the cross-slats. L3:14203, also from layer 6, is apparently an unfinished runner, 10 cm long and 1.7 cm high. — A *wooden cross slat from a toy sledge*, L3:13786, from layer 4, is 7 × 1.3 cm, has its ends pointed, almost like that in I. Pl. 41.7, and has a lashing groove on the upper side. On L3:13403 and L3:13332, both from layer 2, the ends are abruptly narrowed in.

L3:13936 is apparently a small trapezoidal *toy ulo*, being only a flat stone with a natural extension along the back edge, which forms the handle.

L3:13690, from layer 4, is a small *toy baleen snow beater*, 11.5 cm long, with a symmetrically extended butt.

A small *toy soapstone lamp*, L3:13689, from layer 4, is of the type with a ledge, like that shown in I. Pl. 43.10. Two specimens from layer 7 are of a similar shape, except that the ledge is placed nearer to the front edge.

A *toy soapstone cooking pot*, from layer 3, is a four-sided oblong, with the long sides curving outwards. A fragment, found in layer 7, is apparently from a small, shallow, oval, toy pot.

Sundry materials and unidentified objects.

In layer 3 a piece of a red, agate-like stone was found, and in layer 1 a piece of rock crystal, whereas no flint refuse proper was found.

Twenty-two pieces of *worked soapstone* could not be identified.

A large piece of *iron*, L3:14106, was found in layer 6. It is irregularly four-sided, about 13 × 10.5 cm, and 1.4 cm thick. The shape suggests an axe blade, but the stratified structure proves that it is no doubt a large lump of meteoric iron, coarsely hammered when cold. Professor A. Noe-Nygaard, who has most kindly undertaken the analysis, writes about it as follows:

"Regarding the five specimens sent from the National Museum it is possible to say that L3:14106 is no doubt of worked meteoric iron, differing from ordinary iron in that its lamellae (not iron carbide) can be distinctly seen. No "Wiedmanstätter" figures proper can be expected on account of the mechanical treatment.

A very clear Ni-reaction (qual. chemical) strongly supports the assumption that it is meteoric iron."

A total of 152 fragments or unidentifiable objects of *bone* or similar materials were found. Of these L3:13940, from layer 6, shown on Pl. 4.12, is the most remarkable specimen, to a certain extent reminding one of a long foot for a bladder-dart bladder. It is of walrus ivory, 11 cm long and 1.7 cm broad, with one side flattened. At one end there is an extension of the convex side, which again decreases in thickness towards the cuneiform, rounded end. Two rather wide holes lead from the convex to the flat side, on which they are connected by a deep groove. The hole next to the end goes obliquely through the thick part just described, being on the convex side extended into a funnel-shape, so as to receive the end knob of a line which had been passed through the two holes. The other hole is also extended a little on the same side, in a forward direction. The other end is cut off obliquely, giving the object, if placed upon a shaft, a slanting position with an angle of about thirty degrees. There is, however, no indication of how it might have been attached. It seems as if this fore (?) end were damaged.

About 250 unidentifiable objects are of *wood*. Of these only a few deserve a special description. L3:14740, from layer 8, is a flat handle, about 10 × 2.7 × 1.3 cm, of uniform breadth. One end is rounded. At the other end are two pairs of deep lashing notches opposite one another. Marks from pressure on the under side prove that it had been attached to an edge about 1.5 cm broad of an unidentifiable object. — L3:14744, also from layer 8, is a round wooden stick 10.8 cm long, 0.8 cm in diameter, increasing a little in thickness towards the ends which are conically pointed. — L3:14586, from layer 7, is a wooden stick, 6.5 cm long, with an almost semi-circular cross-section, 0.6 cm broad. In the flat side a deep, longitudinal groove has been cut, and the rounded side bears marks of having been wound round with cord—perhaps lashed on to a corresponding half. — L3:14481, also from layer 7, is a piece of wood, made almost into a ball, with a diameter of about 2.2 cm.

Of *baleen lines* with knobs twelve fragments were found in the layers 5—8. To these can be added 23 fragments of *baleen strips*, from the layers 4—8, and 25 unidentifiable pieces of worked baleen, from layers

9*

2—7. Of the latter L3:14097, from layer 6, has the shape of a broad needle, resembling that shown in I. fig. 108.4. It is 20 cm long, and the breadth is 1.7 cm, evenly decreasing towards the point. At the rear end is an oval hole 0.7 cm wide, and a semicircular notch. L3:13728, from layer 4, is an 18 cm long piece of a similar implement of which the point has been cut off. Between the hole and the notch in the rear end there is a groove, indicating that a line had been tied on. These objects may be large trout needles.

Objects of European origin. — In the two uppermost layers several objects of European manufacture were found, of which only characteristic samples were collected: nails, cartridge cases, pieces of glass and earthenware, etc. etc. — A piece of earthenware was also found in layer 3. In layer 5 were found: a brass cartridge case, a piece of thick russet, a piece of faience, and a heavy brass hook. The possibility cannot be excluded, however, that these objects are intrusive, a water stream once having cut deep down into the midden, as mentioned in I. p. 148.

LIST OF QUOTED LITERATURE
(Cf. bibliography in Part II).

BIRKET-SMITH, K.: Ethnography of the Egedesminde District. MoG. Bd. 66. — København 1924.
— Ethnographical Collections from the Northwest Passage. Rep. 5th Thule Exp. Vol. VI, No. 2. — Copenhagen 1945.
BOAS, FR.: The Eskimo of Baffin Land and Hudson Bay. Bull. Amer. Mus. Nat. Hist. XV, Part I. — New York 1901.
COLLINS, H. B.: Archeology of St. Lawrence Island, Alaska. Smithsonian Misc. Coll. Vol. 96, No. 1. — Washington 1937.
GEIST, O. W. and FR. G. RAINEY: Archaeological Excavations at Kukulik. — Washington 1936.
GIDDINGS, J. L.: The Arctic Woodland Culture of the Kobuk River. — Philadelphia 1952.
GLOB, P. V.: Eskimo Settlements in Kempe Fjord and King Oscar Fjord. MoG. Bd. 102, Nr. 2. — København 1935.
HATT, G.: Arktiske Skinddragter i Eurasien og Amerika. — København 1914.
HOFFMAN, W. J.: The Graphic Art of the Eskimos. — Washington 1897.
HOLTVED, E.: Archaeological Investigations in the Thule District. I—II. MoG. Bd. 141, Nr. 1—2. — København 1944.
KNUTH, E.: Et umiak-fund i Peary Land. Fra Nationalmuseets Arbejdsmark, 1951. — København 1951.
LARSEN, H.: Dødemandsbugten. MoG. Bd. 102, Nr. 1. — København 1934.
— and FR. RAINEY: Ipiutak and the Arctic Whale Hunting Culture. Ant. Pap. Amer. Mus. Nat. Hist. Vol. 42. — New York 1948.
MATHIASSEN, TH.: Archæology of the Central Eskimos, I. Rep. 5th Thule Exp. Vol. IV. — Copenhagen 1927.
— Inugsuk. MoG. Bd. 77. — København 1930.
— Ancient Eskimo Settlements in the Kangâmiut Area. MoG. Bd. 91, Nr. 1. — København 1931.
NELSON, E. W.: The Eskimo about Bering Strait. 18th Ann. Rep. Bur. Ethn. — Washington 1899.
RAINEY, FR. G., see GEIST and RAINEY, and LARSEN and RAINEY.
RICHTER, S.: A Contribution to the Archæology of North-East Greenland. Skrifter om Svalbard og Ishavet, Nr. 63. — Oslo 1934.
ROWLEY, G.: The Dorset Culture of the Eastern Arctic. Amer. Anthropologist, N. S. 42. — Washington 1940.

LIST OF ILLUSTRATIONS

		Page
1.	The Nûgdlît glacier. In the foreground two kayak supports	7
2.	Map of the Thule area, showing the position of Nûgdlît	8
3.	Survey plan of the Nûgdlît ruin site	10
4.	Stone rings	12
5.	Plan of house 1, 2 and 3, Nûgdlît	14
6.	Nûgdlît, house 1 after excavation, seen from east	15
7.	Plan of house 4, Nûgdlît	16
8.	Nûgdlît, house 4 before excavation	17
9.	Plan of house 5, Nûgdlît	17
10.	Plan of house 6, Nûgdlît	18
11.	Fire-place in house 6, Nûgdlît	19
12.	Nûgdlît. Plan of house 8 and the passage of the swept away house 14.	20
13.	Plan of house 10, 11 and 16, Nûgdlît	21
14.	Nûgdlît, house 10 after excavation	22
15.	Plan of house 13.A and 13.B, Nûgdlît	23
16.	Plan of house 17, Nûgdlît	26
17.	Plan of house 19, Nûgdlît	27
18.	Plan of house 18, 20 and 21, Nûgdlît	28
19.	Plan of house 22, Nûgdlît	29
20.	Plan of house 23, Nûgdlît	30
21.	Nûgdlît, house 23 after excavation. View through the passage towards the anteroom. To the left the kitchen	31
22.	Plan of house 24.A, 24.B and 28. Nûgdlît	33
23.	Plan of house 25, 26 and 27, Nûgdlît	34
24.	Nûgdlît, house 27 after excavation	35
25.	Kitchen and blubber store in house 28. Nûgdlît	37
26.	Plan of house 29 and ruin 52, Nûgdlît	38
27.	Walrus skull in house 29, Nûgdlît	39
28.	Plan of house 30, Nûgdlît	40
29.	Nûgdlît, house 30 after excavation	41
30.	Nûgdlît, house 31 after excavation	41
31.	Plan of house 31, 32 and 33, Nûgdlît	42
32.	Nûgdlît. The rear part of house 32 after excavation	43
33.	Nûgdlît. Plan of ruin 56, 57 and 58, and the not excavated ruins nr. 61 and 62	47
34.	Plan of ruin 55, 59 and 60, Nûgdlît	48
35.	Nûgdlît. Ruin 59 after excavation	49
36.	Nûgdlît. Ruin 60 after excavation	49
37.	Tent-ring near house 6, Nûgdlît	60
38.	Ornamented harpoon heads from Nûgdlît	62

39. Line buckle of bear shape, from Nûgdlît house 13.B 65
40. Parts of toboggan(?) of baleen, from Nûgdlît house 20 68
41. Fore-end of sledge runner, from Nûgdlît house 6 69
42. Sledge cross slat(?), from house 29, Nûgdlît 70
43. Harpoon rest for umiaq(?), from Nûgdlît house 16 71
44. Boat-hook, from house 6, Nûgdlît 71
45. Stone pestle, from ruin 59, Nûgdlît 75
46. Stone scraper, from house 24.B, Nûgdlît 77
47. Profile of lamp fragment, from Nûgdlît house 26 78
48. Profile of pottery lamp fragment, from Nûgdlît house 31 79
49. Gutskin jacket, L3:12893, from Nûgdlît. (A) front view; (B) side of hood, and shoulder part; (C) under side of sleeve 82
50. Gutskin jacket, L3:12893, from Nûgdlît. Back view 83
51. Gutskin jacket, L3:12894, from Nûgdlît. Front view................. 84
52. Gutskin jacket, L3:12894, from Nûgdlît. (A) back view; (B) side of the hood 84
53. Gutskin jacket, L3:12895, from Nûgdlît. Front view................. 85
54. Gutskin jacket, L3:12895, from Nûgdlît. (A) back view; (B) side of the hood 85
55. Loose hood of birdskin, from Nûgdlît house 28 86
56. Fragment of birdskin trousers(?), from Nûgdlît house 28.............. 87
57. Fragments of boots, from Nûgdlît house 28.......................... 88
58. Boot sole, from house 10, Nûgdlît 89
59. Mitten of bearskin, from Nûgdlît house 26........................... 89
60. Pendant with dot ornament, from Nûgdlît house 28.................. 90
61. Unidentified objects from Nûgdlît.................................... 93
62. Baleen ring of unknown use. Nûgdlît house 26...................... 94
63. Catcher of baleen, from Comer's midden, Thule 117
64. Snow beater of baleen. Comer's midden, Thule...................... 128

PLATES

Plate 1.

Approx. 1:2

		L3:	Nûgdlît:	Ref. p.
1.	Harpoon head	12196	House 13.A	62
2.	—	12901	— 29	61
3.	—	12578	— 24.A+B	61
4.	—	12302	— 16	61
5.	—	12637	— 24.B	61
6.	—	12900	— 29	61
7.	Button with animal heads	12274	— 13.B	90
8.	Animal figure	13107	— 32	91
9.	Swivel	12905	— 29	63
10.	Chain pendant	12735	— 26	91
11.	Mending plug for bladder	12583	— 24.A+B	63
12.	Unknown object of ivory	13156	Ruin 52	91
13.	Pot hook	12269	House 13.B	80
14.	Harpoon head fragment	13184	Ruin 57	62
15.	Stopper for harpoon line	12254	House 13.B	63
16.	Dog figure	12277	— 13.B	91
17.	Pendant	13106	— 32	90
18.	Line buckle, bear head	12733	— 26	65
19.	— — figure	12276	— 13.B	65
20.	Flint side scraper	12678	— 25	77
21.	Plug for towing bladder (?)	13042	— 31	65
22.	Leister-harpoon head (?), baleen	12335	— 16	67
23.	Sinew twister	12907	— 29	66
24.	Socket-piece, for dart (?)	12902	— 29	64
25.	Arrow head	12906	— 29	67
26.	—	12255	— 13.B	67
27.	Knife handle	12908	— 29	72

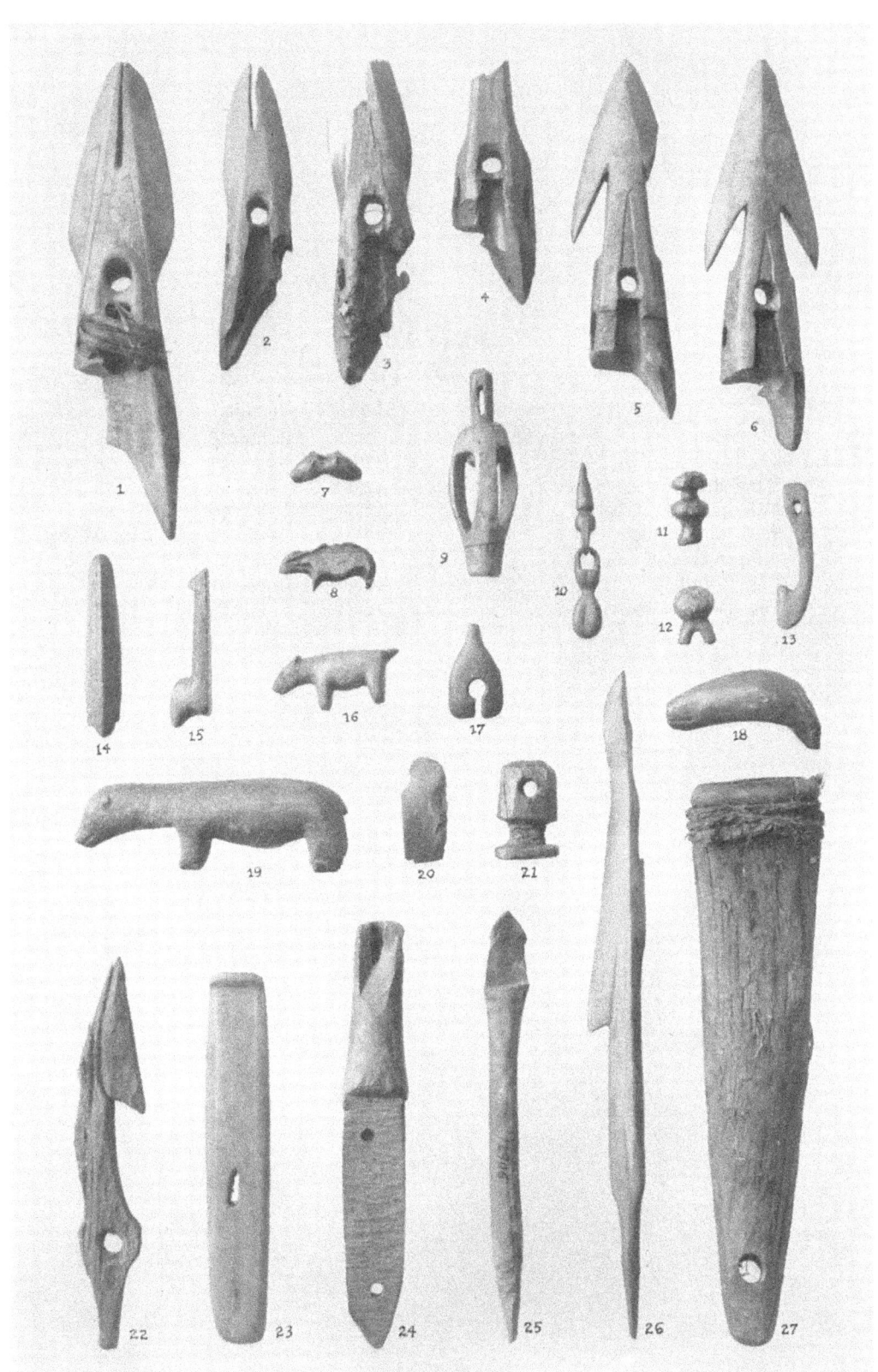

Approx. 1:2.

Plate 2.

Approx. 1:2

	L3:	Nûgdlît:	Ref. p.
1. Ulo handle	12726	House 26	76
2. —	12914	— 29	76
3. Hand drill	12982	— 30	73
4. Fish spoon (?) of baleen	12797	— 26	80
5. Snow knife handle	12418	— 19	72
6. Scraper (?) blade of bone	13156	Ruin 52	93
7. Baleen knife	13065	House 31	73
8. Toy harpoon, baleen	12960	— 29	92

PLATE 2.

Approx. 1:2.

Plate 3.

5:9

		L3:	Comer's midden:	Ref. p.
1.	Knife handle	14568	Layer 7	121
2.	Adze head	14300	— 7	124
3.	Scraper	13971	— 6	124
4.	Lamp trimmer	14195	— 6	126
5.	Two-handed scraper of antler	14529	— 7	124
6.	Toy sealing stool seat	14641	— 7	130
7.	Hand drill (?)	14086	— 6	123
8.	Fish hook	13941	— 6	118
9.	Barb for salmon spear (?)	14585	— 7	116
10.	Baleen comb	14761	— 8	128
11.	Leister prong (?), baleen	14028	— 6	117
12.	Cutting board (?), baleen	14451	— 7	125
13.	Baleen saw	14783	Thule, house 24 I. p. 141	

Plate 4.

Approx. 1:1

		L3:	Comer's midden:	Ref. p.
1.	Mouth-piece for towing bladder	13249	Layer 1	113
2.	— - —	13248	— 1	113
3.	Swivel	13285	— 1	113
4.	Ferrule for whip shank	13257	— 1	119
5.	Chain link	13953	— 6	128
6.	Mending disc(?) of wood	14732	— 8	114
7.	Barb for salmon spear(?)	13305	— 2	116
8.	Tension piece for harpoon line	13246	— 1	113
9.	Toggle	13538	— 3	118
10.	—	13687	— 4	118
11.	Bodkin	13952	— 6	125
12.	Foot for bladder-dart bladder(?)	13940	— 6	131
13.	Leg for kayak rack	14694	— 8	120

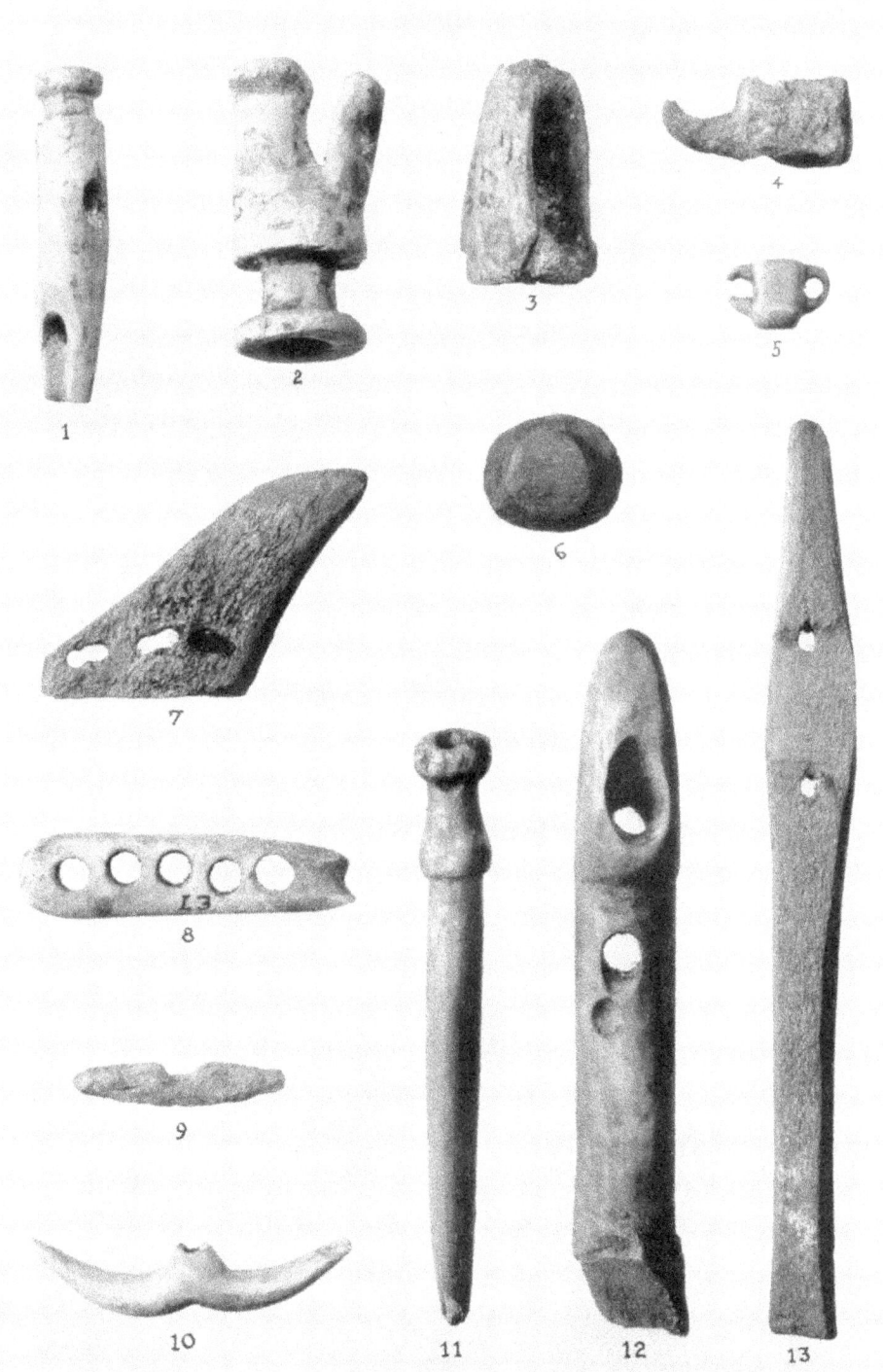

Approx. 1:1.

MONOGRAPHS ON GREENLAND | MEDDELELSER OM GRØNLAND

ABOUT THE SERIES
Monographs on Greenland | Meddelelser om Grønland (ISSN 0025 6676) has published scientific results from all fields of research on Greenland since 1878. The series numbers more than 345 volumes comprising more than 1250 titles.

In 1979 Monographs on Greenland | Meddelelser om Grønland was developed into a tripartite series consisting of Bioscience (ISSN 0106-1054), Man & Society (ISSN 0106-1062), and Geoscience (ISSN 0106-1046).

Monographs on Greenland | Meddelelser om Grønland was renumbered in 1979 ending with volume no. 206 and continued with volume no. 1 for each subseries. As of 2008 the original Monographs on Greenland | Meddelelser om Grønland numbering is continued in addition to the subseries numbering.

Further information about the series, including addresses of the scientific editors of the subseries, can be found at www.mtp.dk/MoG.

MANUSCRIPTS SHOULD BE SENT TO
Museum Tusculanum Press
University of Copenhagen
126 Njalsgade, DK-2300 Copenhagen S
DENMARK
info@mtp.dk | www.mtp.dk
Tel. +45 353 29109 | Fax +45 353 29113
VAT no.: 8876 8418

ORDERS
Books can be purchased online at www.mtp.dk, via order@mtp.dk, through any of our distributors in the US, UK, and France or via online retailers and major booksellers. Museum Tusculanum Press bank details: Amagerbanken, DK-2300 Copenhagen S, BIC: AM BK DK KK, IBAN: DK10 5202 0001 5151 08.

DISTRIBUTORS
USA & Canada: ISBS International Specialized Book Services, 920 NE 58th Ave. Suite 300 - Portland, OR 97213, Phone: +1 800 944 6190 (toll-free), Fax: +1 503 280 8832, orders@isbs.com

United Kingdom: Gazelle Book Services Ltd., White Cross Mills, High Town, GB-Lancaster LA1 4XS, United Kingdom, Phone: +44 1524 68765, Fax: +44 1524 63232, sales@gazellebooks.co.uk

France: Editions Picard, 82, rue Bonaparte, F-75006 Paris, France,
Phone: +33 (0) 1 4326 9778, Fax: +33 1 43 26 42 64,
livres@librairie-picard.fr

www.ingramcontent.com/pod-product-compliance
Lightning Source LLC
Chambersburg PA
CBHW081158020426
42333CB00020B/2549